D0413503

CANADIAN IMMIGRATION MADE EASY

How To Immigrate into Canada (All Classes)
How To Apply
With Settlement Guide & Employment Search Strategies for Skilled Workers

By

Tariq Nadeem

ISBN: 0-9733140-1-X (e-book)
ISBN: 0-9733140-0-1 (Paperback)

This book is printed on acid free paper.

Printed in the United States of America
Bloomington, IN
By arrangements with Self-help Publishers Canada

Acknowledgements

I wish to thank Ms. Irena Valenta of Scarborough North Job Finding Club, who has prepared "Strategizing for Employment in the Canadian Workplace" with the support of Colin Morrison, Executive Director of The Career Foundation and the Programs and Services Team at the Scarborough Office of Human Resources Development Canada (HRDC) for their generous contribution in this publication. Ms. Irena Valenta can be reached by e-mail at: snjfc@careerfoundation.org

I must thank and appreciate the cooperation of Ms. Nicole Hudon of Crown Copyright and Licensing, Communication Canada who has guided me in a professional manner and corrected me on several occasions.

Disclaimer

Her Majesty, her employees and agents, Author and editors shall not be liable for any losses, claims, demands, injuries, causes of action, actions, damages suffered by the user or users of this publication.

Portions of this book have been provided courtesy of Citizenship and Immigration Canada. The Government of Canada does not endorse or support any annotations or commentary included in this publication. These are the sole responsibility and choice of the author.

CONTENTS

CHAPTER - I

CHAPTER - II

WELCOME TO CANADA

GETTING TO KNOW CANADA
BASIC SERVICES 86

WHERE TO BEGIN

CHAPTER - III

WHY STRATEGIZE?

INTRODUCTION

This book features all classes of Canadian immigration under the new Immigration and Refugee Protection Act (IRPA), which was put into effect on June 28, 2002. A brief introduction has been given about every class, which leads to Canadian immigration with respect to eligibility requirements and how to achieve it by visiting the corresponding web link for details about any particular category.

The immigration polices and rules are reviewed from time to time by Citizenship and Immigration Canada (CIC) based on results and objectives. Therefore, CIC constantly updates it's website, ***www.cic.gc.ca,*** to incorporate new changes to deliver up-to-date information to their clients.

In view of the above, a web link has been provided for all the information in this book hence, encouraging readers to extract or verify particular information by visiting the CIC website before taking any action towards filing their application.

Hopefully this approach will provide the latest and up-to-date information to meet your needs when it comes to Canadian Immigration.

The settlement part of this book will provide almost every bit of information, which is necessary for new immigrants to successfully settle within any geographically region of their choice in Canada.

An industry veteran, Ms. Irena Valenta, has designed a strategy for employment search in a Canadian workplace to help foreign trained skilled workers to find employment in a professional and efficient manner.

I believe this book will prove to be an asset for every reader who wishes to start a new life in Canada.

CHAPTER - I

IMMIGRATING TO CANADA

IMMIGRATING TO CANADA

Every year, Canada welcomes thousands of new residents. Coming to Canada as an immigrant is an exciting opportunity, but also a great challenge.

If you are interested in immigrating to Canada, you have a number of options when applying for permanent residence status. Read about these programs and decide which class suits you and your family best.

Immigration Classes

▶ **Skilled Worker Class Immigration**

Canada values the skills and experiences that foreign professionals and workers bring with them. Check to see if your skills and experience qualify you to come to Canada as a skilled worker.

▶ **Business Class Immigration**

Canada has a strong economic culture. If you have experience running or investing in businesses, you may qualify to come to Canada as a business immigrant.

▶ **Family Class Immigration**

Family class immigration reunites families in Canadian homes. Learn how to sponsor your family member or come to Canada as a member of the family class.

▶ **International Adoption**

Adopting children from abroad can be a long process. This is to protect children's rights. Learn about what you need to do to bring an adoptive child to Canada.

▶ **Provincial Nomination**

Most provinces in Canada have programs to encourage immigrants to settle in their province and benefit their economies. Learn about settling in one of Canada's provinces as a provincial nominee.

▶ **Quebec-Selected Immigration**

Quebec is responsible for selecting immigrants who wish to settle in Quebec. Find out how to apply to be selected to settle in Quebec.

IMMIGRATING TO CANADA AS A SKILLED WORKER

Skilled workers are people whose education and work experience will help them find work and make a home for themselves as permanent residents in Canada. Applying to come to Canada as a Skilled Worker is not difficult. You will find all the information and forms you need to make your application at www.cic.gc.ca

Refer to the CIC site often (www.cic.gc.ca). The rules for applying as a Skilled Worker can change. Before you apply, make sure your application follows the current rules.

Canada welcomes skilled worker immigrants. CIC's web site will provide you with helpful information about living and working in the various provinces and regions of Canada.

Will You Qualify As A Skilled Worker?

Skilled workers are people who may become permanent residents because they have the ability to become economically established in Canada.

To be accepted as a Skilled Worker, applicants must:
- Meet the minimum work experience requirements;
- Prove that they have the funds required for settlement; and
- Earn enough points in the six selection factors to meet the pass mark.

The following categories will help you determine if you can apply as Skilled Worker. You can assess your chances of being accepted. Consult each of the following areas for the current regulations.

Six Selection Factors
and Pass Mark

Applications are assessed on **six** selection factors as well as a points system.

- Read about the six selection factors for Skilled Workers
- Learn about how the points system works.
- Check the current pass mark for applications.

These charts show how points are awarded in the six selection factors.

Factor One: Education	Maximum 25
You have a Master's Degree or Ph.D. **and** at least 17 years of full-time or full-time equivalent study.	25
You have two or more university degrees at the bachelor's level **and** at least 15 years of full-time or full-time equivalent study.	22
You have a three-year diploma, trade certificate or apprenticeship **and** at least 15 years of full-time or full-time equivalent study.	22
You have a university degree of two years or more at the bachelor's level and at least 14 years of full-time or full-time equivalent study.	20
You have a two-year diploma, trade certificate or apprenticeship **and** at least 14 years of full-time or full-time equivalent study.	20
You have a one-year university degree at the bachelor's level **and** at least 13 years of full-time or full-time equivalent study.	15
You have a one-year diploma, trade certificate or apprenticeship **and** at least 13 years of full-time or full-time equivalent study.	15
You have a one-year diploma, trade certificate or	12

apprenticeship **and** at least 12 years of full-time or full-time equivalent study.	
You completed high school.	5
Learn more about the <u>specific requirements and definitions of terms</u>. **at:** http://www.cic.gc.ca/english/skilled/qual-5-1.html	

Factor Two: Official Languages	Maximum 24
1st Official Language (English)	
High proficiency (per ability)	4
Moderate proficiency (per ability)	2
Basic proficiency (per ability)	1 to maximum of 2
No proficiency	0
Possible maximum (all 4 abilities)	16
2nd Official Language (French)	
High proficiency (per ability)	2
Moderate proficiency (per ability)	2
Basic proficiency (per ability)	1 to maximum of 2
No proficiency	0
Possible maximum (all 4 abilities)	8
Learn more about the <u>specific requirements and the documents you need</u>. at *http://www.cic.gc.ca/english/skilled/qual-3.html*	

Factor Three: Experience	Maximum 21
1 year	15
2 years	17
3 years	19
4 years	21

Learn more about specific requirements for earning work experience points at: *http://www.cic.gc.ca/english/skilled/qual-5-2.html*

Factor Four: Age	Maximum 10
21 to 49 years at time of application	10
Less 2 points for each year over 49 or under 21	
View the full age chart to determine your points at *http://www.cic.gc.ca/english/skilled/qual-5-3.html*	

Factor Five: Arranged Employment In Canada	Maximum 10
You have a Human Resources Development Canada (HRDC) confirmed offer of permanent employment.	10
You are applying from within Canada and have a temporary work permit that is:	
HRDC confirmed, including sectoral confirmations; or	10
HRDC confirmation exempt under NAFTA, GATS, CCFTA, or significant economic benefit (i.e. intra-company transferee.)	10
Learn more about specific requirements and conditions at. *http://www.cic.gc.ca/english/skilled/qual-5-4.html*	

Factor Six: Adaptability	Maximum 10
Spouse's or common-law partner's education	3 - 5
Minimum one year full-time authorized work in Canada	5
Minimum two years full-time authorized post-secondary study in Canada	5
Have received points under the Arranged Employment in Canada factor	5
Family relationship in Canada	5
Learn more about specific requirements and conditions. *http://www.cic.gc.ca/english/skilled/qual-5-5.html*	

Total	Maximum 100
Pass Mark	75

Selection Criteria	Maximum Points
Education	25
Official languages (English and/or French)	24
Employment experience	21
Age	10
Arranged employment in Canada	10
Adaptability	10
TOTAL	100

Will You Qualify?

1. If your score is the same or higher than the pass mark, then you may qualify to immigrate to Canada as a skilled worker. After reading the information on CIC's Web site, if you wish to apply for immigration, consult the application instructions at: *http://www.cic.gc.ca/english/skilled/how-1.html* (**How to Apply**)

2. If your score is less than the pass mark, you are not likely to qualify to immigrate to Canada as a Skilled Worker. We recommend that you do not apply at this time.

   You may submit a formal application if you believe that there are factors that would show that you are able to become economically established in Canada. Send a detailed letter with your application explaining why you think you are able to become economically established in Canada. Include any documents that support your claim.

Principal Applicant

If you are married or living with a common-law partner, you and your spouse or common-law partner must decide who will be the principal applicant. The other person will be considered the dependant in the applications.

Note: A common-law partner is the person who has lived with you in a conjugal relationship for at least one year. Common-law partner refers to both opposite-sex and same-sex couples.

Use the self-assessment test to help you determine which person would earn the most points. The person who would earn the most points should apply as the principal applicant.

Try the **on-line Self-Assessment** at *http://www.cic.gc.ca/english/skilled/assess/index.html* to see how many points you would earn in the six selection factors explained above.

Things to Consider Before Applying

- Application Fees
- Funds required to settle in Canada
- Medical Examinations
- Whether you should hire someone to represent you
- Choosing a destination in Canada

Application Fees

There are two application fees you will have to pay when you apply to immigrate to Canada as a skilled worker:

1. Application Fee:

This fee must be paid for the principal applicant and any accompanying spouse, common-law partner, and dependant children.

- Pay this when you apply.
- This fee is not refundable.

Find out what the current fees are for Skilled Workers at *http://www.cic.gc.ca/english/applications/fees.html#rprf* ("Other applicants)

2. Right of Permanent Residence Fee:

This fee must be paid for the principal applicant and accompanying spouse or common-law partner.

- Pay this any time while Citizenship and Immigration Canada (CIC) is processing your application. You must pay this before CIC can issue you your permanent residence visa.
- This fee is refundable if:
    - o you cancelled your application;
    - o CIC did not issue your visa to you; or
    - o you did not use your visa.

Find out what the current fees are at *http://www.cic.gc.ca/english/applications/fees.html#rprf*

Additional Fees:

You will have to pay the fees related to obtaining:

- your medical examination;
- police certificates; and
- language testing.

Proof of Funds

The Government of Canada does not provide financial support to new skilled worker immigrants.

You **must** show that you have enough money to support yourself and your dependants after you arrive in Canada. **You cannot borrow this**

money from another person. You must be able to use this money to support your family.

You will need to provide proof of your funds when you submit your application for immigration.

The amount of money that you need to have to support your family is determined by the size of your family.

Number of Family Members	Funds Required (in Canadian dollars)
1	$9,420
2	$11,775
3	$14,645
4	$17,727
5	$19,816
6	$21,905
7 or more	$23,994

You do **not** have to show that you have these funds if you have arranged employment in Canada.

How Much Money Should you Bring?

Find out how much it costs to live where you are planning to settle in Canada.

- Bring as much money as possible to make moving and finding a home in Canada easier.

Disclosure of funds:

If you are carrying more than CDN $10,000, tell a Canadian official when you arrive in Canada. **If you do not tell an official you may be fined or put in prison.** These funds could be in the form of:

- cash;
- securities in bearer form (for example: stocks, bonds, debentures, treasury bills); or
- negotiable instruments in bearer form (for example: bankers' drafts, cheques, travelers' cheques, money orders.)

Medical Examinations

You must pass a medical examination before coming to Canada. Your dependants must also pass a medical examination even if they are not coming with you.

Applications for permanent residence will not be accepted if that person's health:

- is a danger to public health or safety; or
- would cause excessive demand on health or social services in Canada.

Medical Examination Instructions

Instructions on how to take the medical examination will normally be sent to you after you submit your application to the Visa Office.

Validity

You can only use your examination results in your application for 12 months from when you had the examination. If you are not admitted to Canada as a permanent resident within this time, you will be required to undergo another examination.

Authorized Doctors

Your own doctor cannot do the medical examination. You must see a physician on Canada's list of Designated Medical Practitioners at *http://www.cic.gc.ca/english/contacts/medical.html*

Medical Report Procedures

Medical reports and x-rays for the medical examination become the property of the Canadian Immigration Medical Authorities and cannot be returned to you.

The **doctor will not tell you the results** of the medical examination. The doctor will let you know if you have a health-related problem.

The DMP does **not** make the final decision. Citizenship and Immigration Canada will make the final decision on whether or not your medical examination has been passed for immigration purposes.

The Visa Office will tell you in writing if there is a problem with your medical examination.

Whether you need to hire someone to represent you
http://www.cic.gc.ca/english/pub/represent.html

It is **not** necessary to hire a consultant to assist you with your immigration application. The process is simple and easy to follow. All the forms and information you need are available at www.cic.gc.ca. Learn more about:

- Specific conditions that apply only **if you do decide to hire** an agent or consultant.

CHOOSING A DESTINATION IN CANADA

Canada is a large country with many cities and communities. Now that you have decided to come to Canada, you should think about where you want to live. Canada is made up of 10 provinces and three territories, each with different weather, geography, cultures and job opportunities.

When choosing a place to live, you can decide if you want to live near an ocean, near the mountains, on the prairies, in the lake regions or in Canada's arctic shield.

By visiting following province specific websites you will find all kinds of information that you need to know while settling down in any of the following provinces and territories.

- **British Columbia**
  http://www.mcaws.gov.bc.ca/amip/

- **Alberta**
  http://www.learning.gov.ab.ca/welcome/

- **Saskatchewan**
  http://www.iaa.gov.sk.ca/iga/immigration/Immigration.htm

- **Manitoba**
  http://www.gov.mb.ca/labour/immigrate/index.html

- **Ontario**
  http://www.gov.on.ca/citizenship/english/citdiv/immigrat/index.html

- **Quebec**
  http://www.immigration-quebec.gouv.qc.ca/anglais/index.html

- **New Brunswick**
  http://www.gnb.ca/immigration/english/index.htm

- **Nova Scotia**
  http://www.gov.ns.ca/

- **Prince Edward Island**
  http://www.gov.pe.ca/islandlife/

- **Newfoundland and Labrador**
  http://www.gov.nf.ca/

- **Yukon**
  http://www.gov.yk.ca/

- **Northwest Territories**
  http://www.gov.nt.ca/

- **Nunavut**
  http://www.gov.nu.ca/Nunavut/

BUSINESS CLASS IMMIGRATION
http://www.cic.gc.ca/english/business/index.html

Canada has a strong economic culture. If you have experience running or investing in businesses, you may qualify to come to Canada as a business immigrant.

WHO IS A BUSINESS IMMIGRANT?

Business immigrants are people who can invest in, or start businesses in Canada and are expected to support the development of a strong and prosperous Canadian economy. The Business Immigration Programs seek to attract people experienced in business to Canada.

Business immigrants are selected based on their ability to become economically established in Canada.

There are three classes of business immigrants:

Investors
http://www.cic.gc.ca/english/business/invest-1.html

The Immigrant Investor Program seeks to attract experienced persons and capital to Canada. Investors must demonstrate business experience, a minimum net worth of CDN $800,000 and make an investment of CDN $400,000.

Entrepreneurs
http://www.cic.gc.ca/english/business/entrep-1.html

The Entrepreneur Program seeks to attract experienced persons that will own and actively manage businesses in Canada that will contribute to the economy and create jobs. Entrepreneurs must demonstrate business experience, a minimum net worth of CDN $300,000 and are subject to conditions upon arrival in Canada

Self-employed persons
http://www.cic.gc.ca/english/business/self-1.html

Self-employed persons must have the intention and ability to create their own employment. They are expected to contribute to the cultural or athletic life of Canada. They may create their own employment by purchasing and managing a farm in Canada.
The application forms and guide can be downloaded from this site.
http://www.cic.gc.ca/english/applications/business.html

Immigrating to Canada as an Investor

As an investor, you must make a prescribed investment of CDN $400,000. This investment is placed with the Receiver General of Canada.

Participating provinces then use your investment to create jobs and help their economics grow. Citizenship and Immigration Canada (CIC) will return your investment to you, without interest, in approximately five years after you become a permanent resident.

You may finance your investment. CIC has agreements with a number of financial institutions, all of which are members of the Canada Deposit Insurance Corporation (CDIC), (http://www.cdic.ca/?id=100) to facilitate the financing of your investment.

Details for the Investor Program:

▶ **Regulatory Requirements**
http://www.cic.gc.ca/english/business/invest-2.html

As an investor, you must meet the regulatory requirements for the class.

▶ **How to Apply**
http://www.cic.gc.ca/english/business/invest-3.html

▶ **When and How to Pay Your Investment**
  http://www.cic.gc.ca/english/business/invest-4.html

▶ **Application for Business Immigrants**
  http://www.cic.gc.ca/english/applications/business.html

▶ **The Contacts** you need for your application are listed here.
  http://www.cic.gc.ca/english/business/contacts-1.html

▶ **The Fee Schedule** is available with current application fees.
  http://www.cic.gc.ca/english/applications/fees.html

▶ **Business Immigration Program Statistics, 2000** are
  published for your information.
  http://www.cic.gc.ca/english/business/bus-stats2000.html

▶ **Other Links**
  Start here to learn more about investing and living in Canada.
  http://www.cic.gc.ca/english/business/links.html

The province of Quebec has it's own Immigrant Investor Program.
Learn about investing and living in Quebec from the Quebec
Immigration Office at: *http://www.cic.gc.ca/english/contacts/que.html*

Immigrating to Canada
as an Entrepreneur

To qualify as an entrepreneur, you must have business experience. This means that you must have managed and controlled a percent of equity of a qualifying business. Entrepreneurs must have a legally obtained net worth of at least CDN $300,000.

When you immigrate to Canada as an entrepreneur, you must have the intention and the ability to control a percentage of equity of a qualifying Canadian business. You must provide active and ongoing management of the qualifying Canadian business. Your business must create at least one new full-time job for a Canadian citizen or permanent resident. You must meet these requirements **within three years** of becoming a permanent resident.

Before your immigrant visa is issued, you are required to sign a statement that you intend and will be able to meet the conditions of permanent residence.

Details of the Entrepreneur Program:

▶ **Regulatory Requirements**
http://www.cic.gc.ca/english/business/entrep-2.html
As an entrepreneur, you must meet the regulatory requirements for the entrepreneur class.

▶ **How to Apply**
http://www.cic.gc.ca/english/business/entrep-3.html

▶ **Application for Business Immigrants**
http://www.cic.gc.ca/english/applications/business.html

▶ **The Fee Schedule** is available with current application fees.
http://www.cic.gc.ca/english/applications/fees.html

▶ **Business Immigration Program Statistics, 2000** are published for your information.
http://www.cic.gc.ca/english/applications/fees.html

▶ **The Contacts** you need for your application are listed here.
http://www.cic.gc.ca/english/business/contacts-2.html

▶ **Entrepreneur Counselling and Monitoring Guides**
http://www.cic.gc.ca/english/business/entrep-4.html. These guides contain the information you require after you become a permanent resident of Canada.

▶ **Other Links**
http://www.cic.gc.ca/english/business/links.html
Start here to learn more about living in Canada.

Immigrating to Canada as a Self-employed Person

As a self-employed person, you must have relevant experience in cultural activities, athletics or farm management. You must also have the intention and ability to establish a business that will, at a minimum, create employment for yourself. You must make a significant contribution to cultural activities or athletics or purchase and manage a farm in Canada.

No immigration conditions are imposed on this class. You must have enough money to support yourself and your family members after you arrive in Canada.

Details of the Self-Employed Person Program:

▶ **Regulatory Requirements**
   http://www.cic.gc.ca/english/business/self-2.html
   As a self-employed person, you must meet the regulatory requirements for the class.

▶ **How to Apply**
   http://www.cic.gc.ca/english/business/self-3.html

▶ **Application for Business Immigrants**
   http://www.cic.gc.ca/english/applications/business.html

▶ **The Fee Schedule** is available with current application fees. *http://www.cic.gc.ca/english/applications/fees.html*

▶ **Business Immigration Program Statistics, 2000** are published for your information.
   http://www.cic.gc.ca/english/business/bus-stats2000.html

▶ **The Contacts** you will need for your application are listed here. *http://www.cic.gc.ca/english/business/contacts-2.html*

▶ **Other Links** Start here to learn more about living in Canada. *http://www.cic.gc.ca/english/business/links.html*

FAMILY CLASS IMMIGRATION
http://www.cic.gc.ca/english/sponsor/index.html

Family class immigration reunites families in Canadian homes. Learn how to sponsor your family member or come to Canada as a member of the family class.

Canadian citizens and permanent residents living in Canada, 18 years of age or older, may sponsor close relatives or family members who want to become permanent residents of Canada. Sponsors must promise to support the relative or family member and their accompanying family members for a **period of three to 10 years** (*http://www.cic.gc.ca/english/sponsor/support.html*) to help them settle in Canada.

If you live in Quebec, please contact **Quebec Immigration**

(*http://www.immigration-quebec.gouv.qc.ca/anglais/index.html*) for information on how to sponsor a relative or family member. The *Canada-Quebec Accord* provides information on Quebec's responsibilities for immigration.

You can sponsor relatives or family members from abroad if they are:

- spouses, common-law or conjugal partners 16 years of age or older;
- parents and grandparents;
- dependent children, including adopted children;
- children under 18 years of age whom you intend to adopt;
- brothers, sisters, nephews, nieces or grandchildren who are orphans; under the age of 18 and not married or in a common-law relationship; or
- you may also sponsor one relative of any age if you do not have an aunt, uncle or family member from the list above whom you could sponsor or who is already a Canadian citizen, Indian or permanent resident.

A son or daughter is dependent when the child:

- is under the age of 22 and does not have a spouse or common-law partner;
- is a full time student and is substantially dependent on a parent for financial support since before the age of 22, or since becoming a spouse or common-law partner (if this happened before age 22); or
- is financially dependent on a parent since before the age of 22 because of a disability.

Spouse or Common-Law Partner in Canada Class

You may also sponsor a spouse or common-law partner from within Canada if they have been living with you in Canada and have maintained their legal temporary status. Sponsorship of a spouse or common-law partner includes their dependent children whether inside or outside of Canada.

Sponsoring a Relative or Family Member

If you want to sponsor any of the above listed relatives or family members, you may have to meet certain income requirements. If you have previously sponsored relatives or family members who have received social assistance, you may not be allowed to sponsor another person. Sponsorship is a considerable commitment so you should take this obligation seriously.

To sponsor a relative or family member you must sign an Undertaking with the Minister of Citizenship and Immigration. You must also sign a Sponsorship Agreement with your relative or family member that outlines your mutual commitments to each other.

Sponsoring a Relative or Family Member

To adopt a child from another country you must go through both the adoption process and the sponsorship and immigration process. Learn more about international adoptions at
http://www.cic.gc.ca/english/sponsor/adopt-1.html

Applying as a Sponsored Immigrant

If you wish to become a permanent resident of Canada, your relative or family member in Canada must first apply to sponsor you. You must be one of the relatives or family members listed above to be eligible for sponsorship.

Both you and your sponsor need to sign a Sponsorship Agreement. The Agreement outlines your mutual obligations to each other. Your sponsor must promise to support you and your family members financially for three to 10 years so that you will not need to apply for social assistance. You must promise to make every effort to become self-supporting (unless you are elderly.)

There is lots of help out there for those looking for work. Find out more about <u>Working in Canada</u>.

http://www.cic.gc.ca/english/skilled/work-1.html

Applications for Sponsorship and Immigration to Canada from Abroad

Before your relative or family member can immigrate to Canada, you must sponsor that person. Your relative or family member must then apply for immigration. Learn more and print the information guides and applications *http://www.cic.gc.ca/english/sponsor/out.html* you need for sponsorship and immigration.

Applications for Sponsorship and Immigration from Within Canada

In some cases, you may sponsor a spouse or common-law partner who is already living with you in Canada. Learn more and print the information guides and applications
http://www.cic.gc.ca/english/sponsor/in.html you need for sponsorship and immigration.

Changes to Submission of Family Class Applications

On February 17, 2003, Citizenship and Immigration Canada (CIC) introduced a new application kit and submission process. This affects Family Class sponsorship and permanent resident applications for spouses, common-law partners, conjugal partners and dependent children applying outside of Canada.

The new process does not apply if you are sponsoring any other family members or to applications for the Spouse/Common-Law Partner in Canada Class.

On June 28, 2002, CIC changed the application submission process for the Family Class, to allow clients to submit joint applications, including both the sponsorship application and the permanent resident application.

To build on the efficiency of this new process, CIC has introduced a process, which **allows clients to complete the medical examination prior to submitting the joint application**. The improved process will assist in faster processing of applications made on behalf of spouses, common-law partners, conjugal partners or dependent children.

The new kit includes instructions on how your spouse, common-law partner, conjugal partner or dependent child may take the medical examination before the joint application is submitted to Case Processing Centre (CPC) Mississauga.

The new applications are available on this Web site for download *http://www.cic.gc.ca/english/applications/fc.html* and through CIC Call Centres *http://www.cic.gc.ca/english/contacts/call.html*. You will find that many of the documents required for submission with the previous applications are also required for the new one. We will be updating the information about the new application procedure on this Web site, so please visit often.

The new application is part of CIC's commitment to finding new ways to improve the efficiency and to ensure timely processing of permanent resident applications to reunite family members.

Q. What is an up-front medical examination?

A. An up-front medical examination allows applicants (your spouse, common-law partner, conjugal partner, or dependent children) to take the medical examination before the applications for sponsorship and permanent residence are submitted to Case Processing Centre (CPC) Mississauga.

With the examinations done at the beginning of the process, Citizenship and Immigration Canada (CIC) will be able to process the permanent residence application faster.

Q. What are the benefits of the up-front medical examination?

A. When CIC tested the joint application and up-front medical examination process, processing times was reduced by over 50% for routine cases.

Q. Why is CIC changing the way these types of applications are handled?

A. The new application and submission process will make the processing of applications more streamlined and faster. It is the next step in improvements to the processing of sponsorships and permanent residence applications made on behalf of spouses, common-law partners, conjugal partners and dependent children. The first step was the introduction of the joint application kit on June 28th, 2002.

Q. When does this new application process start?

A. The new application process came into effect on February 17, 2003. The new application kits are available on the CIC Web site and from the Call Centres.

Q. Are all sponsorship and permanent residence applications for spouses, common-law partners, conjugal partners and dependent children automatically subject to the new processing system?

A. No. The new application process is only for spouses, common-law partners, conjugal partners and dependent children applying for permanent residence **outside of Canada**.

Q. So, what exactly is the entire new process for applying as a spouse, common-law partner, conjugal partner or dependent child from outside of Canada?

A. The sponsor will receive the new joint application, including the sponsorship and permanent residence applications, and instructions for completing the medical examination. The sponsor must complete the sponsorship portion and the relative (and the relative's family members) must complete the permanent residence portion.

Once all of the documents have been gathered to support the applications, the relative being sponsored (and the relative's dependent children, if applicable) should contact a Designated Medical Practitioner (DMP), which is a doctor who is authorized by CIC to perform the medical examination, to take the medical examination.

After the medical examination is completed, the DMP will give the person examined a document showing that the medical examination has been done. The relative must then send this document (one for each family member) to the sponsor along with the completed permanent residence application and all supporting documents.

The sponsor will put together the permanent residence application, including all supporting documents, the proof that the medical examination has been done, the sponsorship application and the sponsorship documents, and then submits the package to CPC-Mississauga.

CPC-Mississauga will first determine if the sponsor is eligible to sponsor and then will send the permanent residence package by courier to the Visa Office. The Visa Office will then process the permanent residence application. By the time the Visa Office receives the permanent residence application, the medical assessment should also have arrived at the Visa Office--unless there was a medical condition that required further assessment.

The Visa Office will then process the permanent residence application and decide if a permanent resident visa may be issued.

Q. Do I use the new application process if I live in Quebec?

A. Yes. You and your relative will also benefit from the new application process. However, as per the Canada-Quebec Accord, the province of Quebec has a role in determining the eligibility of sponsors living Quebec. The Quebec process is initiated after CPC-Mississauga has completed its assessment of your ability to meet federal sponsorship requirements. CPC-Mississauga will courier your relative's permanent residence application to the Visa Office and will advise Quebec of the federal decision, so that the Quebec process can be started. If you meet Quebec's eligibility criteria, then the Ministère des Relations avec les citoyens et de l'immigration (MRCI) will issue an Engagement and Certificat de sélection du Quebec (CSQ) to you. A copy of each document will be sent to the Visa Office for inclusion in their process.

Q. Does my spouse, common-law partner, conjugal partner or dependent child, have to do an up-front medical examination?

A. Up-front medical examinations are not mandatory. However, only applications with up-front medical examinations will benefit from quicker processing times.

Q. What happens if the up-front medical examination results expire because of delays?

A. CIC has instituted processing changes and given priority processing to these applications to minimize situations in which medical results will expire before the application process can be completed. In non-routine cases, where the medical results expire, a new medical examination will need to be done.

Note: medical results are valid for one year from the date of the medical examination.

Q. How and when will my spouse and I find out about the results of the medical exam?

A. The results of the medical examination will be sent to the Visa Office that will be processing your spouse's permanent residence application. Therefore, it is very important to correctly fill out the form that starts the medical examination process to ensure that the medical results go to the correct Visa Office.

Q. What happens if my spouse or dependent children fail the medical examination?

A. The Visa Office will advise your spouse or dependent child if they fail the medical examination.

Q. Why are adopted children not included in this initiative?

A. Adopted children are not included in this initiative because there are already priority-processing instructions for dealing with these cases, which work very well.

Q. I recently mailed in an old joint sponsorship application to CPC-Mississauga. What should I do now?

A. The old application will not be accepted by CPC-Mississauga, as the new application process came into effect on February 17th, 2003.

Q. I have completed and am ready to submit my sponsorship and my common-law partner's permanent residence application, which were done with the old applications. Do I have to get a new kit and do everything all over again?

A. Yes. The new application process came into effect on February 17th, 2003.

Q. Where can I get more information on the new kit?

A. Updates on the new application and submission process are available on CIC's site. You may order the applications from the Call Centres or download and print them directly from CIC's site.

Q. Can other people in Family Class (parents, grandparents) get up-front medical examinations too?

A. No. The up-front medical examination process is only available to spouses, common-law partners and dependent children. If any other members of the Family Class (i.e., parents, grandparents) use the up-front medical examination process, the medical results will not be valid and will have to be re-done.

This is because under the new immigration legislation, (IRPA) medical requirements for spouses, common-law partners, conjugal partners and dependent children are different from the medical requirements that must be met for other members of the Family Class.

Q. Will my application be rejected if I do not use the new application?
    A. After February 17th, 2003 the new applications must be used.

Q. I have just completed the old joint application and am waiting for my spouse to complete and send me the permanent resident portion of the application. Should I tell my spouse not to send it in because there will be a new application kit?

A. Your spouse should complete and return to you the permanent residence portion to submit it to CPC-Mississauga using the new application, which came into effect on February 17th, 2003

Please note that the applications are available on CIC's site and can be downloaded and printed directly by your spouse.

International Adoption
http://www.cic.gc.ca/english/sponsor/adopt-1.html

Adopting children from abroad can be a long process. This is to protect children's rights. Learn about what you need to do to bring an adoptive child to Canada.

International Adoption

Canadian law allows you to adopt a child from another country if you are a Canadian citizen or permanent resident. To bring your adoptive child to Canada, you must sponsor the child for immigration. You can start sponsoring a child as soon as you decide to adopt or you can wait until after you have found a child and have started the adoption process.

There are two processes that you must go through when you adopt a child from another country: the adoption process and the immigration sponsorship process. **You need to know about both**.

The Adoption Process:

Adoptions are the responsibility of the provinces in Canada. You need to have a Home Study done, usually by your province, before Citizenship and Immigration Canada (CIC) processes your application for sponsorship.

You will have to comply with the adoption laws of the child's country of origin. You must also comply with the laws of your province. Make sure you are familiar with all of the legal requirements relevant to you before beginning the adoption process.

Find out what you must do to <u>adopt a child from another country</u> from your province at this link

http://www.cic.gc.ca/english/sponsor/adopt-3.html

The Hague Convention governs international adoptions in some cases. Before you begin your adoption process, <u>find out if the Convention will apply to you</u> here *http://www.cic.gc.ca/english/sponsor/adopt-5.html*

The Immigration Process:

As an adoptive parent of a child from another country, you must <u>apply to sponsor the child</u> *http://www.cic.gc.ca/english/applications/family.html* for permanent residence in Canada. You may apply for citizenship on the child's behalf after the child is in Canada and has permanent resident status.

CIC will request a letter of consent from your province showing that your province agrees to the adoption. The immigration visa will only be issued after the immigration mission in the child's country of origin receives this letter from your province.

For more information on bringing a child from another country to Canada, please see *International Adoption and the Immigration Process*. *http://www.cic.gc.ca/english/sponsor/adopt-4.html*

Frustrated with time-consuming processes that seem bureaucratic?

These procedures help to protect children's best interests. The only way around this frustration is to please be patient.

Provincial Nomination
http://www.cic.gc.ca/english/skilled/provnom/index.html

Most provinces in Canada have programs to encourage immigrants to settle in their province and benefit their economies. Learn about settling in one of Canada's provinces as a provincial nominee.

Provincial Nomination

Most provinces in Canada have an agreement with the Government of Canada that allows them to play a more direct role in selecting immigrants who wish to settle in that province. If you wish to immigrate to one of Canada's provinces as a Provincial Nominee, you must first apply to the province where you wish to settle. The province will consider your application based on their immigration needs and your genuine intention to settle there.

Before applying to immigrate to Canada, Provincial Nominees must complete the provincial nomination process. **Contact the province for more information** at:
http://www.cic.gc.ca/english/skilled/provnom/contacts.html

Note: After a province has nominated you, you have to make a separate application to Citizenship and Immigration Canada (CIC) for permanent residence. A CIC officer will assess your application based on Canadian immigration regulations.

Provincial Nominees **are not** assessed on the six selection factors of the Federal Skilled Workers Program.

Provincial Nominee Program - Contact Information

If you wish to come to Canada as a Provincial Nominee, you must first apply to the province to be nominated for immigration. Citizenship and Immigration Canada will process your application for permanent residence after the province sends a Certificate of Provincial Nomination to the Visa Office where you will send your forms.

Contact the provinces for more information on their Provincial Nominee Programs.

Alberta
Provincial Nominee Program
Economic Immigration
Alberta Economic Development
4th Floor, Commerce Place
10155-102 Street
Edmonton, Alberta
T5J 4L6
www.alberta-canada.com/pnp

British Columbia
Provincial Nominee Program
Ministry of Community, Aboriginal & Women's Service
P.O. Box 9915 Stn Prov Gov
Victoria, British Columbia
V8W 9V1
www.pnp.mi.gov.bc.ca

Manitoba
Provincial Nominee Program
Immigration Promotion & Recruitment Branch

Labour and Immigration Manitoba
9th Floor, 213 Notre Dame Avenue
Winnipeg, Manitoba
R3B 1N3
http://www.gov.mb.ca/labour/immigrate/english/immigration/1.html

New Brunswick
Provincial Nominee Program
Training and Employment Development
P.O. Box 6000
Fredericton, New Brunswick
E3B 5H1
www.gnb.ca/immigration/english/index.htm

Newfoundland and Labrador
Provincial Nominee Program
Industry, Trade and Technology
Confederation Building
West Block, 4th Floor
P.O. Box 8700
St. John's, Newfoundland
A1B 4J6
www.gov.nf.ca/itrd/prov_nominee.htm

Nova Scotia
Provincial Nominee Program
The Office of Economic Development
World Trade and Convention Centre
1800 Argyle Street
P.O. Box 519
Halifax, Nova Scotia
B3J 2R7
www.gov.ns.ca

Prince Edward Island
Provincial Nominee Program
Immigration and Investment Division
94 Euston Street, 2nd floor

Charlottetown, Prince Edward Island
C1A 7M8
www.gov.pe.ca

Saskatchewan
Provincial Nominee Program
Dept. of Government Relations and Immigration
Immigration Branch
2nd Floor - 1919 Saskatchewan Drive
Regina, Saskatchewan
S4P 3V7
www.immigrationsask.gov.sk.ca

Yukon
Provincial Nominee Program
Business Immigration, Industry Development
Business, Tourism and Culture
P.O. Box 2703
Whitehorse, Yukon
Y1A 2C6
www.btc.gov.yk.ca

Quebec-Selected Immigration

Quebec is responsible for selecting immigrants who wish to settle in Quebec. Find out how to apply to be selected to settle in Quebec at, *http://www.cic.gc.ca/english/skilled/quebec/index.html*

Immigrating to Quebec as a Skilled Worker

The Quebec government and the Government of Canada have an agreement that allows Quebec to select immigrants who best meet its immigration needs. Under the Canada-Quebec Accord on Immigration, Quebec is able to establish its own immigration requirements and select immigrants who will adapt well to living in Quebec.

To come to Canada as a Quebec Skilled Worker, you must first apply to the Quebec government for a *Certificat de selection du Québec*. Visit the Quebec Immigration Web site for more information. *http://www.immigration-quebec.gouv.qc.ca/anglais/immigration/permanent-worker/selection-admission.html*

Note: After you have been selected by Quebec, you have to make a separate application to Citizenship and Immigration Canada (CIC) for permanent residence. A CIC officer will assess your application based on Canadian immigration regulations.

Quebec Skilled Workers **are not** assessed on the six selection factors of the Federal Skilled Workers Program.

What Happens After You Apply

You can follow the progress of your application after you have submitted it. Find out what happens with your application after you give it to your local visa office. While you are waiting for a decision about your application, you may want to find out more about what it means to be a permanent resident of Canada. Start here to learn about:

The Application Assessment Process

A Visa Office will process your application. The Visa Office may process your application differently depending on your application and the Visa Office. Some processing steps are common to all Visa Offices.

After you submit your application, a Citizenship and Immigration Canada (CIC) officer will check to see that you submitted everything with your application. The officer will make sure that you:

- completed your application form correctly;
- paid your application fee correctly; and
- included all supporting documentation.

If your application is not complete, CIC will return it to you without starting to process it.

Your Visa Office will send you a letter when they receive your completed application. The letter will tell you what you need to do and what happens next.

Processing Time

The length of time it takes to process your application can be different in each mission or Visa Office. Visit the mission Web site *http://www.cic.gc.ca/english/offices/missions.html* (if available) where you submitted your application for more information on how long it might take to process your application.

You may be able to speed up the process by:

- making sure all the necessary information is included with your application;

- notifying the Visa Office of any changes to the information on your application;

- avoiding unnecessary enquiries to the Visa Office;

- making sure the photocopies and documents you provide are clear and readable;

- providing certified English or French translations of documents, where indicated; and

- applying from a country where you are a citizen or permanent resident.

Your application will be delayed if the Visa Office has to take extra steps to assess your case. Your application will take longer if:

- there are criminal or security problems with your application;
- your family situation is not clear because of a situation such as a divorce or adoption that is not yet complete or child custody issues that have not been resolved; or

- the local Visa Office has to consult with other CIC offices in Canada or abroad.

Checking the Status of Your Application

Once you have received notice from our office that your application has been received, you can check the status of your application online at: *http://www.cic.gc.ca/english/e-services/index.html*

You may use this on-line service to view the status of your application if you have:

- sponsored a member of the family class
- applied for permanent residence as a member of the family class
- applied for permanent residence from within Canada as the spouse or common-law partner of a Canadian citizen or permanent resident
- applied as an independent immigrant (for applicants who applied before January 1, 2002), a Québec skilled worker, a provincial nominee, a federal skilled worker, an investor, an entrepreneur, or a self-employed person .

Before using this service, please be sure to have a copy of all the documents you have received relating to your application(s):

These may include **one or more** of the following:

- a copy of your application
- your financial receipt(s) (IMM 5401)
- any official document issued to you by Citizenship and Immigration Canada

WHO MAY REPRESENT YOU

A representative may be a lawyer, a consultant or any other person, including a friend, whom you hire for a fee or ask to help you do any of the following at no charge: (1) apply for permanent residence or a temporary stay in Canada; (2) submit a refugee claim; (3) appear in front of an adjudicator; (4) appeal a decision; (5) apply for citizenship; or (6) request information on matters dealing with the *Immigration Act* or the *Citizenship Act.*

What you should know before seeking the services of someone to help with your application

Do you need a representative?

- Citizenship and Immigration Canada (CIC) does not require you to have a representative. We have tried to make our application kits as simple as possible so that you can complete them yourself. You can get additional information on how to complete an application from the CIC Web site or from a CIC Call Centre.

- If you decide to use the services of a representative, you are free to do so.

- CIC treats all applicants equally and does not provide preferential service to applicants with representatives.

Who can act as a representative?

- Anyone can act as a representative.
- Only lawyers licensed to practice in Canada can represent you at the Federal Court.
- CIC can provide information on your file only to people who are either (1) Canadian citizens, (2) permanent residents of Canada or (3) physically present in Canada. Representatives who live outside Canada and are neither Canadian citizens nor permanent residents might be unable to help you.
- Volunteer and non-governmental organizations that deal with immigrants may provide free services.

General points

- CIC cannot recommend representatives or vouch for their honesty or skills. It is your responsibility to make sure that the representative you choose is ethical and competent to perform the services required. You should not be afraid to ask the representative (whether a lawyer or a consultant) for references or for other proof that he or she has the necessary skills.

- Beware of representatives who claim that you will get a visa, obtain citizenship or benefit from special treatment from the Canadian government by using their services. CIC is not associated with any representatives.

- Be cautious when dealing with foreign-based representatives. Such companies or individuals may be outside the reach of Canadian law, and there may be no protection or remedy available in Canada to a dissatisfied client.

Lawyers

- Provincial regulatory bodies regulate lawyers practicing in Canada. Only a lawyer who is a member in good standing of a provincial or territorial law society may practice law. The law societies regulate lawyers and can investigate complaints against members, impose discipline and provide financial compensation to clients who are victims of negligence or misconduct.

- If you live in Canada and you want to hire a lawyer, call the law society of the province or territory in which you live for the names of lawyers. In many cases, you can consult a lawyer free of charge for half an hour before deciding if you want to hire him or her. However, in some cases, a fee may be charged for the consultation.

Immigration consultants

- The federal or provincial governments of Canada do not regulate immigration consultants.

- Find out if the consultant (whether he or she is in Canada or overseas) belongs to a professional association in Canada and ask about his or her experience with immigration or citizenship matters.

- Call the Better Business Bureau (BBB) to find out if the consultant has a satisfactory rating. Business people who fail to respond to letters of complaint sent to the BBB receive an unsatisfactory rating.

Dealing with representatives

- CIC requires your written authorization in order to release information to your representative.

- You may give your own mailing address or the mailing address of your representative as a point of contact for CIC. If you choose to give your representative's address, all correspondence from CIC, including notices for interviews, requests for information, medical forms and visas, will be sent to the representative.

- If you change representatives or stop using their services, you must cancel your authorization in writing to CIC or CIC will continue dealing with them. If you hire a new representative, you will have to provide a new authorization to CIC.

- Make sure that the representative who helps you with your application is willing to be identified as your representative.

Information given to CIC must be truthful

- Submitting false or misleading information to CIC can lead to the refusal of your application, the cancellation of your visa, the revocation of your citizenship, your deportation from Canada, and criminal charges being laid against you.

- You are responsible for any documents you submit to CIC or that your representative submits on your behalf.

Where to go for help if things go wrong

CIC cannot help you if you have a dispute with your representative as it is a private matter between the two of you. However, you may write to the CIC office dealing with your case or to the following address to inform CIC of the situation:

Citizenship and Immigration Canada
Social Policy and Programs
Selection Branch
Jean Edmonds Tower North, 7th Floor
300 Slater Street
Ottawa, Ontario KIA 1L1

Note: You should file a complaint with the proper authorities as soon as possible if you encounter serious difficulties with your representative as limitation periods may apply.

If your representative is a lawyer practicing in Canada

- Address your complaint to the law society of the province or territory where your lawyer practices. Law societies impose a code of conduct on their members to try to protect the public interest. They have rules for disciplining lawyers and compensating clients. You may be able to obtain financial compensation from the law society's insurance fund.

If your representative is a consultant practicing in Canada

- If your consultant is a member of a professional association in Canada, file a complaint with that association.

- If your consultant is not a member of any association, you might ask the consumer protection office in your province or territory for advice. Some associations might offer to contact the consultant to seek a solution.

- You can report your problem to the Better Business Bureau in the province or territory where your representative works. The BBB might contact your representative to try to resolve the issue for you.

If your representative is either a lawyer or an immigration consultant practicing in Canada

- If you believe your representative has committed an offense in the course of representing you, you should go to the local police or to the Royal Canadian Mounted Police.

- If you are in Canada and you wish to recover money you paid for services you did not get, you can file a lawsuit in small claims court. You do not need a lawyer to do so, but you will have to pay a small fee.

- Legal Aid services are available throughout Canada for people who cannot afford to pay for legal assistance. Contact them to see if you qualify for assistance.

If your representative's place of business is abroad

- If your representative is not a Canadian citizen or a permanent resident of Canada, you should present your complaint to the appropriate authorities overseas. The Canadian government cannot get involved in the dispute.

CIC Call Centre

Montréal	(514) 496-1010
Toronto	(416) 973-4444
Vancouver	(604) 666-2171
Elsewhere in Canada	1-888-242-2100

YOU ASKED ABOUT IMMIGRATION AND CITIZENSHIP

In order to ensure the latest and up-to-date delivery of information on Canadian immigration and citizenship you are encouraged to read CIC's guide "**You Asked About Immigration And Citizenship**" from time to time:

http://www.cic.gc.ca/english/pub/you-asked/index.html

This guide provides information to the public on CIC's policy as well as the process to follow for immigrating and/or obtaining citizenship to Canada.

"**You Asked About Immigration And Citizenship**" will provide you up-to-date information on the following topics.

AN INTRODUCTION TO CITIZENSHIP AND IMMIGRATION CANADA

- The Immigration and Refugee Protection Act
- What are CIC's objectives?
- How many people work for CIC and where are they?
- What other departments and agencies are involved in citizenship and immigration programs?
- How can I get current information about immigration and citizenship?

IMMIGRATION

- Overview & Objective
- The Annual Report to Parliament and immigration plan
- What role do the provinces and territories play in immigration?
- How many immigrants come to Canada every year?
- How many visitors come to Canada every year?

IMMIGRATION OPERATIONS

- How should I apply?
- Do people have to pay fees to apply to come to Canada?
- What is the right of permanent residence fee?
- Why has CIC changed the way it serves clients?
- What are some of the changes to CIC's services?
- What is the Permanent Resident Card?
- What are the rights and obligations of permanent residents?

IMMIGRATION OPERATIONS IN CANADA

- What is the role of the Case Processing Centres?
- How do I pay the fees?
- How does CIC deliver the immigration program abroad?
- Where should I apply?
- How long does it take CIC to process an application?
- What are the medical requirements?
- Where are the immigration offices in Canada?
- What is the role of the Case Processing Centres?
- How do I pay the fees?

IMMIGRATION OPERATIONS ABROAD

- How does CIC deliver the immigration program abroad?
- Where should I apply?
- How long does it take CIC to process an application?
- What are the medical requirements?

IMMIGRATION AND REFUGEE BOARD

- What does the Immigration and Refugee Board do?
- Refugee Protection Division
- What happens at a refugee protection hearing?
- Refugee Appeal Division

- Immigration Division
- Immigration Appeal Division

FEDERAL-PROVINCIAL AGREEMENTS

- What are provincial nominees?
- Which provinces and territories have immigration
- agreements with the federal government?
- The Canada-Quebec Accord
- Who needs Quebec's approval?
- What settlement services does Quebec provide?

IMMIGRATING TO CANADA

- What are the categories of permanent residents?
- How can I apply to immigrate to Canada?
- Can I include my family members on my application?

FAMILY CLASS IMMIGRATION

- Who is eligible for sponsorship in the family class?
- Can I sponsor a family member already living in Canada?
- What is a common-law partner?
- What is a conjugal partner?
- Can I sponsor any other relatives?
- How can I adopt a foreign child?
- What is the Hague Convention?
- What are the requirements for adoption?
- Can I sponsor a child whom I have already adopted outside Canada?
- Can I sponsor a child to be adopted in Canada?
- Are there different procedures in Quebec?
- Can I sponsor a member of the family class?
- Can I sponsor my family members if I live outside Canada?

- How long am I financially responsible for my relatives?
- Who is not eligible to sponsor a member of the family class?
- How do I apply to sponsor a member of the family class?
- What happens if I don't meet the sponsorship requirements?
- Can I withdraw my sponsorship later?
- How can I find out whether I qualify for immigration to Canada?
- Skilled workers
- Are qualifications earned outside the country recognized in Canada?
- What is the "point" system?
- What criteria apply to applications already in progress on June 28, 2002?

ECONOMIC CLASSES

- How can I find out whether I qualify for immigration to Canada?
- **Skilled workers**
- Are qualifications earned outside the country recognized in Canada?
- What is the "point" system?
- What criteria apply to applications already in progress on June 28, 2002?
- **Business immigrants**
- Do I qualify as a business immigrant?
- How do I apply?
- Business applicants destined for Quebec
- Provincial and territorial nominees

REFUGEES

- How many refugees does Canada accept annually?
- Who are Convention refugees?

- Do other people need protection?
- How are refugees selected abroad?
- Who may sponsor a refugee?
- How can I sponsor a refugee?
- What assistance does the government give refugees?

REFUGEE PROTECTION IN CANADA

- What is a claim for refugee protection in Canada?
- Who decides that a person is a refugee or protected person?
- Who is not eligible to have a refugee protection claim considered?
- What happens at a refugee hearing?
- What is meant by cessation or vacation?
- What happens when a person is accepted as a refugee?
- What happens if the refugee claim is refused?
- What is a Pre-Removal Risk Assessment?
- When can a refugee protection claimant be removed?
- What rights do refugee protection claimants have?

SETTLEMENT PROGRAMS AND SERVICES

- How does Canada help newcomers adapt to living in Canada?
- What settlement programs and services are available?

TEMPORARY RESIDENTS

- Do I need a temporary resident visa?
- What do visa officers consider when assessing
- applications for temporary resident visas?

FOREIGN STUDENTS

- What do I need if I want to study in Canada?
- Am I allowed to work while studying in Canada?

TEMPORARY FOREIGN WORKERS

- What do I need if I want to work in Canada?
- How can I hire a foreign worker?
- How is the government making it easier for high-tech
- companies to hire highly skilled foreign workers?
- What is the Live-in Caregiver Program?
- What are the requirements for live-in caregivers?

Business Visitors

- What are the temporary worker provisions of free trade agreements?

- **North American Free Trade Agreement**

ENFORCEMENT

- What activities are involved in immigration enforcement?
- Who is admissible to Canada?
- Who is inadmissible to Canada?
- What control measures does CIC use overseas?
- What measures does CIC take to combat people smuggling?
- What are background checks?
- Can a criminal ever be considered rehabilitated?
- What role do transportation companies play in preventing illegal migrants from coming to Canada?
- How do immigration officials control people arriving at the border?
- Are there any measures to stop people from abusing the refugee protection system?
- What is a temporary resident permit?
- What happens at an admissibility hearing?
- When can a person be detained?
- What happens when people receive a removal order?

- How many people are actually removed from Canada?
- What are the different kinds of removal orders?
- Are family members included in removal orders?

APPEALS

- Who has a right of appeal under immigration law?
- Who does not have a right of appeal?

QUESTIONS ABOUT STATUS

- Can I change my status after I arrive in Canada as a visitor?
- If I want to leave Canada, how can I maintain my permanent resident status?
- What does Canadian citizenship mean?
- What are my rights as a Canadian?

CITIZENSHIP

- What docs Canadian citizcnship mcan?
- How many people become Canadian citizens every year?
- What are my rights as a Canadian?
- What are my responsibilities as a Canadian?

BECOMING A CANADIAN CITIZEN

- How can I become a Canadian citizen?
- Can I apply in person?
- How do children become citizens?
- How long does it take?
- How much does it cost?
- How do I get an application form?
- How do I fill out the application form?
- Do I get credit for time I spent in Canada before becoming a permanent resident?

- Can I apply for citizenship now, even though I will not have enough residence until next month?
- Can I apply even if I have been temporarily absent from Canada?
- Do I have to apply separately for my children?
- What documents will I need?
- What kinds of photographs are acceptable?

THE CITIZENSHIP TEST

- How long will it be before I am called to write the test?
- What does the test involve?
- What happens if I do not pass the test?
- What if I cannot attend the test session?
- I have a visual, learning or hearing disability. Can I get assistance to take the test?
- Can I reapply if I fail both the test and the oral interview?
- Is my fee refunded if I am not approved for citizenship?
- Does my elderly relative have to learn everything?

THE CITIZENSHIP CEREMONY

- How long will I wait between my test and the ceremony?
- Must my children come to the citizenship ceremony?
- What if I am unable to attend the ceremony?
- What will happen during the ceremony?
- Does my adopted child automatically become a Canadian citizen?

CRIMINAL RECORDS

- Can I become a citizen if I have had problems with the police

OTHER COMMONLY ASKED QUESTIONS
ABOUT CANADIAN CITIZENSHIP

- Can I have dual citizenship?
- If I was born overseas to a Canadian citizen, am I automatically a Canadian citizen?
- Do I become a Canadian when I marry a Canadian?
- Will I lose my citizenship if I live outside Canada for an extended period?
- Can I resume my citizenship?
- Where can I learn more about Canadian citizenship?
- Immigration Fees

FACTS & FIGURES 2001
Immigration Overview

IMMIGRATION REPORT CARD, 2001

IMMIGRANTS	PLANNED RANGE		ACTUAL LANDINGS	DIFFERENCE*
	LOWER	UPPER	IN 2001	%
Immediate Family	42,000	45,000	45,383	1%
Parents and Grandparents	15,000	16,000	21,261	33%
Total Family	**57,000**	**61,000**	**66,644**	**9%**
Skilled Workers	100,500	113,300	137,085	21%
Business Immigrants	15,000	16,000	14,580	-9%
Provincial/Territorial Nominees	1,400	1,400	1,274	-9%
Total Economic	**116,900**	**130,700**	**152,939**	**17%**
Other**	**4,000**	**4,000**	**2,828**	**-29%**
Total Other	**4,000**	**4,000**	**2,828**	**-29%**
Total Immigrants	**177,900**	**195,700**	**222,411**	**14%**
REFUGEES				
Government Assisted Refugees	7,300	7,300	8,693	19%
Privately Sponsored Refugees	2,800	4,000	3,570	-11%
Refugees Landed in Canada	10,000	15,000	11,891	-21%
Dependants Abroad***	2,000	3,000	3,740	25%
Total Refugees	**22,100**	**29,300**	**27,894**	**-5%**
Total Planned	**200,000**	**225,000**	**250,305**	**11%**

Backlog	N/A	N/A	41	
Not stated	N/A	N/A	0	
Total	**200,000**	**225,000**	**250,346**	

Where the planned levels are expressed as ranges, the percentage difference is expressed in terms of the ceiling level of the specified range.

** Other - includes Live-in Caregivers, Post Determination Refugee Claimants, Deferred   Removal Orders, Retirees.
*** Dependants (of a refugee landed in Canada) who live abroad

IMMIGRATION BY LEVEL
(Principal Applicants and Dependants)

IMMIGRANTS	1999		2000		2001	
	#	%	#	%	#	%
Spouse	32,823	17.28	35,246	15.51	37,709	15.06
Parents and Grandparents	14,485	7.63	17,753	7.81	21,261	8.49
Others	7,958	4.19	7,542	3.32	7,674	3.07
Total Family	**55,266**	**29.10**	**60,541**	**26.64**	**66,644**	**26.62**
Skilled Workers	92,437	48.67	118,509	52.13	137,085	54.76
Business Immigrants	13,015	6.85	13,660	6.01	14,580	5.82
Provincial/Territorial Nominees	477	0.25	1,253	0.55	1,274	0.51
Total Economic	**105,929**	**55.77**	**133,422**	**58.69**	**152,939**	**61.09**
Live-in Caregivers	3,260	1.72	2,783	1.22	2,623	1.05
Post-Determination Refugee Claimants	189	0.10	163	0.07	82	0.03
Deferred Removal Orders	833	0.44	297	0.13	123	0.05
Retirees	9	0.00	0	0.00	0	0.00

Total Other	4,291	2.26	3,243	1.42	2,828	1.13
Total Immigrants	165,486	87.13	197,206	86.75	222,411	88.84
Government Assisted Refugees*	7,444	3.92	10,666	4.69	8,693	3.47
Privately Sponsored Refugees	2,330	1.23	2,912	1.28	3,570	1.43
Refugees Landed in Canada	11,792	6.21	12,990	5.71	11,891	4.75
Dependants Abroad**	2,808	1.48	3,490	1.54	3,740	1.49
Total Refugees	24,374	12.84	30,058	13.22	27,894	11.14
Total Immigrants/Refugees	189,860	99.97	227,264	99.97	250,305	99.98
Backlog	61	0.03	48	0.02	41	0.02
Not Stated	1	0.00	1	0.00	0	0.00
Total	189,922	100	227,313	100	250,346	100

- Includes Kosovo refugees who arrived in 1999 as part of a special movement and who obtained permanent resident status in 2000.

** Dependants (of a refugee landed in Canada) who live abroad.

IMMIGRATION BY PROVINCE AND CENSUS METROPOLITAN AREA
(Principal Applicants and Dependants)

CENSUS AREA	1999 #	1999 %	2000 #	2000 %	2001 #	2001 %
St. John's	315	0.17	290	0.13	294	0.12
Other Newfoundland	100	0.05	120	0.05	110	0.04
Total Newfoundland	415	0.22	410	0.18	404	0.16
Total Prince Edward Island	125	0.07	192	0.08	134	0.05
Halifax	1,310	0.69	1,318	0.58	1,381	0.55
Other Nova Scotia	291	0.15	273	0.12	327	0.13
Total Nova Scotia	1,601	0.84	1,591	0.70	1,708	0.68
Saint John	162	0.09	173	0.08	148	0.06
Other New Brunswick	501	0.26	585	0.26	653	0.26
Total New Brunswick	663	0.35	758	0.34	801	0.32
Québec	1,554	0.82	1,405	0.62	1,829	0.73
Montréal	24,943	13.13	28,139	12.38	32,366	12.93
Ottawa - Hull (QC)	730	0.38	684	0.30	585	0.23
Other Quebec	1,858	0.98	2,196	0.97	2,648	1.06
Total Quebec	29,085	15.31	32,424	14.27	37,428	14.95
Ottawa - Hull (ON)	6,577	3.46	7,772	3.42	8,448	3.37
Toronto	84,476	44.48	110,059	48.42	125,061	49.96
Hamilton	2,751	1.45	3,167	1.39	2,767	1.11
London	1,563	0.82	1,973	0.87	1,955	0.78
Other Ontario	8,643	4.55	10,352	4.55	10,194	4.07
Total Ontario	104,010	54.76	133,323	58.65	148,425	59.29
Winnipeg	3,003	1.58	3,700	1.63	3,742	1.49
Other Manitoba	698	0.37	906	0.40	832	0.33
Total Manitoba	3,701	1.95	4,606	2.03	4,574	1.82
Regina	535	0.28	673	0.30	535	0.21
Saskatoon	802	0.42	786	0.35	776	0.31

Other Saskatchewan	388	0.20	429	0.19	398	0.16
Total Saskatchewan	**1,725**	**0.90**	**1,888**	**0.84**		**0.68**
Calgary	6,817	3.59	8,469	3.73	10,169	4.06
Edmonton	3,852	2.03	4,313	1.90	4,580	1.83
Other Alberta	1,390	0.73	1,537	0.68	1,622	0.65
Total Alberta	**12,059**	**6.35**	**14,319**	**6.31**	**16,371**	
Vancouver	32,378	17.05	33,292	14.65	34,165	13.65
Victoria	743	0.39	917	0.40	950	0.38
Other British Columbia	2,955	1.56	3,163	1.39	3,151	1.26
Total British Columbia	**36,076**	**19.00**	**37,372**	**16.44**	**38,266**	**15.29**
Total Yukon		**0.04**	**60**	**0.03**	**67**	**0.03**
Total Northwest Territories	**54**	**0.03**	**82**	**0.04**	**90**	**0.04**
Total Nunavut	**10**	**0.01**	**9**	**0.00**	**6**	**0.00**
Not stated	319	0.17	279	0.12	363	0.15
Total	**189,922**	**100**		**100**	**250,346**	**100**

IMMIGRATION BY SOURCE AREA
(Principal Applicants and Dependants)

	1999		2000		2001	
REGION	**#**	**%**	**#**	**%**	**#**	**%**
Africa and the Middle East	33,490	17.63	40,815	17.96	48,078	19.20
Asia and Pacific	96,437	50.78	120,539	53.03	132,711	53.01
South and Central America	15,221	8.01	16,944	7.45	20,129	8.04
United States	5,528	2.91	5,814	2.56	5,894	2.35
Europe and the United Kingdom	38,930	20.50	42,885	18.87	43,204	17.26
Not stated	316	0.17	316	0.14	330	0.13
Total	**189,922**	**100**	**227,313**	**100**	**250,346**	**100**

IMMIGRATION BY TOP TEN SOURCE COUNTRIES
(Principal Applicants and Dependants)

	1999			2000			2001		
COUNTRY	#	%	Rank	#	%	Rank	#	%	Rank
China	29,112	15.33	1	36,715	16.15	1	40,296	16.10	1
India	17,429	9.18	2	26,086	11.48	2	27,812	11.11	2
Pakistan	9,295	4.89	3	14,182	6.24	3	15,339	6.13	3
Philippines	9,170	4.83	4	10,086	4.44	4	12,903	5.15	4
Korea	7,216	3.80	5	7,626	3.35	5	9,604	3.84	5
U.S.A	5,528	2.91	7	5,814	2.56	7	5,894	2.35	6
Iran	5,907	3.11	6	5,608	2.47	8	5,736	2.29	7
Romania	3,461	1.82	14	4,425	1.95	11	5,585	2.23	8
Sri Lanka	4,723	2.49	9	5,841	2.57	6	5,514	2.20	9
U.K	4,478	2.36	10	4,647	2.04	10	5,345	2.14	10
Taiwan	5,464	2.88	8	3,511	1.54	14	3,111	1.24	19
Yugoslavia	1,490	0.70	29	4,720	2.08	0	2,786	1.11	22
Total for Top Ten Only	98,322	51.78		121,328	53.38		134,028	53.54	
Total Other Countries	91,600	48.22		105,985	46.62		116,318	46.46	
Total	189,922	100		227,313	100		250,346	100	

MONTREAL BY LEVEL
(Principal Applicants and Dependants)

	1999		2000		2001	
IMMIGRANTS	#	%	#	%	#	%
Spouse	4,425	17.74	4,812	17.10	4,970	15.36
Parents and Grandparents	841	3.37	932	3.31	1,116	3.45
Others	1,153	4.62	1,079	3.83	1,182	3.65
Total Family	**6,419**	**25.73**	**6,823**	**24.24**	**7,268**	**22.46**
Skilled Workers	9,030	36.20	11,152	39.63	15,195	46.95
Business Immigrants	3,233	12.96	3,486	12.39	4,387	13.55
Provincial/Territorial Nominees	2	0.01	1	0.00	6	0.02
Total Economic	**12,265**	**49.17**	**14,639**	**52.02**	**19,588**	**60.52**
Live-in Caregivers	377	1.51	265	0.94	206	0.64
Post-Determination Refugee Claimants	67	0.27	47	0.17	14	0.04
Deferred Removal Orders	173	0.69	64	0.23	13	0.04
Total Other	**617**	**2.47**	**376**	**1.34**	**233**	**0.72**
Total Immigrants	**19,301**	**77.37**	**21,838**	**77.60**	**27,089**	**83.70**
Government Assisted Refugees	520	2.08	627	2.23	496	1.53
Privately Sponsored Refugees	107	0.43	145	0.52	175	0.54
Refugees Landed in Canada	3,953	15.85	4,083	14.51	3,410	10.54
Dependants Abroad*	1,057	4.24	1,443	5.13	1,193	3.69
Total Refugees	**5,637**	**22.60**	**6,298**	**22.39**	**5,274**	**16.30**
Total Immigrants/Refugees	**24,938**	**99.97**	**28,136**	**99.99**	**32,363**	**100**
Backlog	5	0.02	3	0.01	3	0.01
Total	**24,943**	**100**	**28,139**	**100**	**32,366**	**100**

* Dependants (of a refugee landed in Canada) who live abroad.

MONTREAL BY TOP TEN SOURCE COUNTRIES
(Principal Applicants and Dependants)

COUNTRY	1999			2000			2001		
	#	%	Rank	#	%	Rank	#	%	Rank
China	1,715	6.88	2	2,677	9.51	2	3,570	11.03	1
France	2,708	10.86	1	3,056	10.86	1	3,060	9.45	2
Morocco	1,253	5.02	4	1,871	6.65	4	2,914	9.00	3
Algeria	1,577	6.32	3	2,000	7.11	3	2,458	7.59	4
Haiti	1,166	4.67	5	1,214	4.31	5	1,735	5.36	5
Romania	985	3.95	6	1,142	4.06	8	1,563	4.83	6
Lebanon	630	2.53	11	707	2.51	10	1,018	3.15	7
India	911	3.65	8	1,169	4.15	7	1,014	3.13	8
Pakistan	822	3.30	9	801	2.85	9	1,008	3.11	9
Sri Lanka	786	3.15	10	1,191	4.23	6	808	2.50	10
Korea,	953	3.82	7	676	2.40	11	608	1.88	11
Total for Top Ten Only	12,876	51.62		15,828	56.24		19,148	59.15	
Total Other Countries	12,067	48.38		12,311	43.76		13,218	40.85	
Total	24,943	100		28,139	100		32,366	100	

TORONTO BY LEVEL
(Principal Applicants and Dependants)

	1999		2000		2001	
IMMIGRANTS	**#**	**%**	**#**	**%**	**#**	**%**
Spouse	13,550	16.04	15,441	14.03	16,433	13.14
Parents and Grand-parents	6,958	8.24	8,900	8.09	11,359	9.08
Others	3,554	4.21	3,403	3.09	3,443	2.75
Total Family	**24,062**	**28.49**	**27,744**	**25.21**	**31,235**	**24.97**
Skilled Workers	47,564	56.30	67,485	61.32	78,557	62.81
Business Immigrants	3,377	4.00	3,909	3.55	4,462	3.57
Provincial/Territorial Nominees	17	0.02	64	0.06	91	0.07
Total Economic	**50,958**	**60.32**	**71,458**	**64.93**	**83,110**	**66.45**
Live-in Caregivers	662	0.78	585	0.53	623	0.50
Post-Determination Refugee Claimants	65	0.08	61	0.06	41	0.03
Deferred Removal Orders	528	0.63	189	0.17	87	0.07
Total Other	**1,255**	**1.49**	**835**	**0.76**	**751**	**0.60**
Total Immigrants	**76,275**	**90.30**	**100,037**	**90.90**	**115,096**	**92.02**
Government Assisted Refugees	1,090	1.29	1,809	1.64	1,437	1.15
Privately Sponsored Refugees	876	1.04	1,206	1.10	1,300	1.04
Refugees Landed in Canada	5,067	6.00	5,500	5.00	5,412	4.33
Dependants Abroad*	1,115	1.32	1,469	1.33	1,785	1.43
Total Refugees	**8,148**	**9.65**	**9,984**	**9.07**	**9,934**	**7.95**
Total Immigrants/Refugees	**84,423**	**99.95**	**110,021**	**99.97**	**125,030**	**99.97**
Backlog	52	0.06	38	0.03	31	0.02
Not stated	1	0.00	0	0.00	0	0.00
Total	**84,476**	**100**	**110,059**	**100**	**125,061**	**100**

- Dependants (of a refugee landed in Canada) who live abroad.

TORONTO BY TOP TEN SOURCE COUNTRIES
(Principal Applicants and Dependants)

	1999			2000			2001		
COUNTRY	#	%	Rank	#	%	Rank	#	%	Rank
China	13,701	16.22	1	18,551	16.86	1	21,487	17.18	1
India	9,127	10.80	2	15,836	14.39	2	17,596	14.07	2
Pakistan	6,511	7.71	3	10,754	9.77	3	11,590	9.27	3
Philippines	3,286	3.89	5	4,031	3.66	5	6,016	4.81	4
Korea	3,003	3.55	7	3,536	3.21	6	4,682	3.74	5
Sri Lanka	3,590	4.25	4	4,237	3.85	4	4,277	3.42	6
United Arab Emirates	1,222	1.45	16	2,258	2.05	8	3,341	2.67	7
Iran	3,136	3.71	6	3,033	2.76	7	2,974	2.38	8
Saudi Arabia	1,071	1.27	18	1,464	1.33	17	2,603	2.08	9
Romania	1,384	1.64	15	1,911	1.74	13	2,445	1.96	10
Russia	2,263	2.68	8	2,149	1.95	9	2,429	1.94	12
Jamaica	1,085	2.35	0	2,068	1.88	10	2,336	1.87	13
United States	1,857	2.20	10	1,981	1.80	12	1,896	1.52	15
Total for Top Ten Only	48,459	57.36		66,453	60.38		77,011	61.58	
Total Other Countries	36,017	42.64		43,606	39.62		48,050	38.42	
Total	84,476	100		110,059	100		125,061	100	

VANCOUVER BY LEVEL
(Principal Applicants and Dependants)

IMMIGRANTS	1999 #	1999 %	2000 #	2000 %	2001 #	2001 %
Spouse	4,867	15.03	4,563	13.71	4,912	14.38
Parents and Grandparents	2,995	9.25	3,258	9.79	3,599	10.53
Others	821	2.54	623	1.87	656	1.92
Total Family	8,683	26.82	8,444	25.37	9,167	26.83
Skilled Workers	16,974	52.42	18,067	54.27	18,759	54.91
Business Immigrants	3,594	11.10	3,401	10.22	3,402	9.96
Provincial/Territorial Nominees	10	0.03	11	0.03	18	0.05
Total Economic	20,578	63.55	21,479	64.52	22,179	64.92
Live-in Caregivers	1,246	3.85	970	2.91	801	2.34
Post-Determination Refugee Claimants	18	0.06	31	0.09	10	0.03
Deferred Removal Orders	77	0.24	37	0.11	17	0.05
Retirees	9	0.03	0	0.00	0	0.00
Total Other	1,350	4.18	1,038	3.11	828	2.42
Total Immigrants	30,611	94.55	30,961	93.00	32,174	94.17
Government Assisted Refugees	739	2.28	1,037	3.11	793	2.32
Privately Sponsored Refugees	268	0.83	205	0.62	237	0.69
Refugees Landed in Canada	570	1.76	905	2.72	746	2.18
Dependants Abroad*	190	0.59	181	0.54	215	0.63
Total Refugees	1,767	5.46	2,328	6.99	1,991	5.82
Total Immigrants/Refugees	32,378	100	33,289	99.99	34,165	100
Backlog	0	0.00	2	0.01	0	0.00
Not stated	0	0.00	1	0.00	0	0.00
Total	32,378	100	33,292	100	34,165	100

* Dependants (of a refugee landed in Canada) who live abroad.

VANCOUVER BY TOP TEN SOURCE COUNTRIES
(Principal Applicants and Dependants)

COUNTRY	1999			2000			2001		
	#	%	Rank	#	%	Rank	#	%	Rank
China, Republic	8,077	24.95	1	9,483	28.48	1	9,518	27.86	1
India	3,438	10.62	3	3,826	11.49	2	3,914	11.46	2
Philippines	2,579	7.97	4	2,619	7.87	3	3,125	9.15	3
Korea, Republic	2,001	6.18	5	1,994	5.99	5	2,656	7.77	4
Taiwan	3,508	10.83	2	2,174	6.53	4	1,861	5.45	5
Iran	1,440	4.45	6	1,221	3.67	6	1,227	3.59	6
United Kingdom	693	2.14	9	632	1.90	9	764	2.24	7
United States	745	2.30	8	724	2.17	8	679	1.99	8
Pakistan	555	1.71	10	630	1.89	10	642	1.88	9
Hong Kong	1,303	4.02	7	933	2.80	7	623	1.82	10
Total for Top Ten Only	24,339	75.17		24,236	72.79		25,009	73.21	
Total Other Countries	8,039	24.83		9,056	27.21		9,156	26.79	
Total	32,378	100		33,292	100		34,165	100	

FAMILY CLASS BY TOP TEN SOURCE COUNTRIES
(Principal Applicants and Dependants)

COUNTRY	1999			2000			2001		
	#	%	Rank	#	%	Rank	#	%	Rank
India	9,539	17.26	1	12,010	19.84	1	12,627	18.95	1
China Republic	5,560	10.06	2	5,741	9.48	2	6,472	9.71	2
United States	2,948	5.33	4	3,169	5.23	4	3,601	5.40	3
Philippines	4,031	7.29	3	3,380	5.58	3	3,395	5.09	4
Pakistan	2,636	4.77	5	2,533	4.18	5	3,219	4.83	5
Jamaica	1,813	3.28	6	1,684	2.78	7	1,980	2.97	6
Vietnam, Republic	1,323	2.39	9	1,708	2.82	6	1,972	2.96	7
Sri Lanka	1,487	2.69	7	1,625	2.68	8	1,781	2.67	8
United Kingdom	1,438	2.60	8	1,388	2.29	9	1,556	2.33	9
Guyana	1,101	1.99	10	1,066	1.76	11	1,309	1.96	10
Hong Kong	1,058	1.91	12	1,182	1.95	10	898	1.35	16
Total for Top Ten Only	31,876	57.66		34,420	56.83		37,912	56.87	
Total Other Countries	23,391	42.34		26,123	43.17		28,734	43.13	
Total	55,267	100		60,543	100		66,646	100	

Canadian Immigration Made Easy

REFUGEE CLASS BY TOP TEN SOURCE COUNTRIES
(Principal Applicants and Dependants)

COUNTRY	1999 #	1999 %	1999 Rank	2000 #	2000 %	2000 Rank	2001 #	2001 %	2001 Rank
Afghanistan	1,816	7.44	3	2,537	8.44	3	2,916	10.45	1
Sri Lanka	2,611	10.70	2	3,235	10.76	2	2,504	8.98	2
Pakistan	1,088	4.46	7	1,237	4.11	5	2,111	7.57	3
Yugoslavia	629	2.58	13	3,834	12.75	1	1,745	6.25	4
Iran	1,447	5.93	4	1,503	5.00	4	1,474	5.28	5
Colombia	169	0.69	29	783	2.60	12	1,281	4.59	6
India	697	2.86	10	1,110	3.69	7	1,153	4.13	7
Iraq	915	3.75	8	982	3.27	8	1,076	3.86	8
Sudan	398	1.63	15	651	2.16	14	1,038	3.72	9
Congo	696	2.85	11	951	3.16	9	928	3.33	10
Somalia	1,381	5.66	5	1,211	4.03	6	828	2.97	11
Bosnia-Herzegovina	2,698	11.06	1	839	2.79	10	639	2.29	13
Croatia	1,187	4.87	6	797	2.65	11	357	1.28	18
Algeria	743	3.05	9	703	2.34	13	282	1.01	21
Total for Top Ten Only	14,583	59.78		17,439	58.00		16,226	58.16	
Total Other Countries	9,810	40.22		12,633	42.00		11,673	41.84	
Total	24,393	100		30,072	100		27,899	100	

BUSINESS CLASS BY TOP TEN SOURCE COUNTRIES
(Principal Applicants)

COUNTRY	1999			2000			2001		
	#	%	Rank	#	%	Rank	#	%	Rank
China	478	13.14	3	899	23.41	1	1,301	31.87	1
Korea	710	19.51	1	653	17.00	2	507	12.42	2
Taiwan	538	14.78	2	314	8.17	3	306	7.50	3
Pakistan	90	2.47	9	113	2.94	9	223	5.46	4
Iran	171	4.70	5	182	4.74	5	200	4.90	5
Hong Kong	339	9.32	4	242	6.30	4	139	3.41	6
United Kingdom	123	3.38	8	109	2.84	10	117	2.87	7
Netherlands	126	3.46	7	115	2.99	8	110	2.69	8
India	66	1.81	12	122	3.18	7	97	2.38	9
United Arab Emirates	44	1.21	15	90	2.34	12	92	2.25	10
Germany	152	4.18	6	130	3.38	6	89	2.18	11
Switzerland	78	2.14	10	54	1.41	14	36	0.88	18
Total for Top Ten Only	2,805	77.08		2,879	74.95		3,092	75.75	
Total Other Countries	834	22.92		962	25.05		990	24.25	
Total	3,639	100		3,841	100		4,082	100	

BUSINESS CLASS BY TOP TEN SOURCE COUNTRIES
(Principal Applicants and Dependants)

	1999			2000			2001		
COUNTRY	#	%	Rank	#	%	Rank	#	%	Rank
China	1,517	11.66	3	2,845	20.83	1	4,191	28.74	1
Korea, Republic	2,703	20.77	1	2,467	18.06	2	1,918	13.16	2
Taiwan	2,091	16.07	2	1,203	8.81	3	1,186	8.13	3
Pakistan	383	2.94	9	447	3.27	8	960	6.58	4
Iran	655	5.03	5	709	5.19	5	737	5.05	5
Hong Kong	1,101	8.46	4	794	5.81	4	473	3.24	6
Netherlands,	465	3.57	6	462	3.38	7	408	2.80	7
United Arab Emirates	192	1.48	15	358	2.62	10	391	2.68	8
United Kingdom	413	3.17	8	356	2.61	11	389	2.67	9
India	214	1.64	13	474	3.47	6	328	2.25	10
Germany	429	3.30	7	369	2.70	9	231	1.58	11
Switzerland	231	1.77	10	147	1.08	18	101	0.69	23
Total for Top Ten Only	9,988	76.74		10,128	74.14		10,981	75.30	
Total Other Countries	3,027	23.26		3,532	25.86		3,599	24.70	
Total	13,015	100		13,660	100		14,580	100	

SKILLED WORKERS BY TOP TEN SOURCE COUNTRIES
(Principal Applicants)

	1999			2000			2001		
COUNTRY	#	%	Rank	#	%	Rank	#	%	Rank
China	10,070	24.24	1	12,759	24.49	1	13,340	22.66	1
India	3,443	8.29	2	5,745	11.03	2	5,934	10.08	2
Pakistan	2,240	5.39	3	3,962	7.60	3	3,304	5.61	3
Philippines	926	2.23	11	1,718	3.30	5	2,729	4.64	4
France	2,135	5.14	4	2,356	4.52	4	2,428	4.13	5
Korea,	1,225	2.95	6	1,348	2.59	7	2,047	3.48	6
Morocco	606	1.46	16	1,065	2.04	9	1,883	3.20	7
Romania	1,133	2.73	8	1,465	2.81	6	1,871	3.18	8
United Kingdom	1,210	2.91	7	1,307	2.51	8	1,548	2.63	9
U.A.E	434	1.04	20	786	1.51	13	1,294	2.20	10
Iran	1,290	3.11	5	1,051	2.02	10	1,071	1.82	12
Russia	1,037	2.50	10	916	1.76	11	975	1.66	14
Taiwan	1,108	2.67	9	720	1.38	16	565	0.96	19
Total for Top Ten Only	24,891	59.93		32,776	62.91		36,378	61.81	
Total Other Countries	16,645	40.07		19,326	37.09		22,482	38.19	
Total	41,536	100		52,102	100		58,860	100	

SKILLED WORKERS BY TOP TEN SOURCE COUNTRIES
(Principal Applicants and Dependants)

COUNTRY	1999 #	1999 %	1999 Rank	2000 #	2000 %	2000 Rank	2001 #	2001 %	2001 Rank
China	21,260	22.99	1	27,410	23.12	1	28,816	21.02	1
India	6,903	7.46	2	12,403	10.46	2	13,649	9.95	2
Pakistan	5,013	5.42	3	9,921	8.37	3	9,012	6.57	3
Philippines	2,190	2.37	12	4,010	3.38	5	6,980	5.09	4
Korea	3,901	4.22	4	4,342	3.66	4	6,854	5.00	5
Romania	2,527	2.73	9	3,387	2.86	7	4,409	3.22	6
U.A.E	1,429	1.55	16	2,607	2.20	9	3,964	2.89	7
France	3,230	3.49	5	3,588	3.03	6	3,691	2.69	8
United Kingdom	2,526	2.73	10	2,786	2.35	8	3,266	2.38	9
Morocco	1,186	1.28	19	1,992	1.68	15	3,221	2.35	10
Russia	2,748	2.97	8	2,268	1.91	11	2,546	1.86	12
Iran	3,091	3.34	6	2,551	2.15	10	2,527	1.84	13
Taiwan	2,914	3.15	7	1,874	1.58	16	1,492	1.09	20
Total for Top Ten Only	54,113	58.50		73,005	61.58		83,862	61.16	
Total Other Countries	38,365	41.50		45,536	38.42		53,257	38.84	
Total	92,478	100		118,541	100		137,119	100	

PROVINCIAL NOMINEES BY PROVINCE
(Principal Applicants and Dependants)

	1999		2000		2001	
PROVINCE	#	%	#	%	#	%
Newfoundland	0	0.00	0	0.00	36	2.83
Nova Scotia	0	0.00	0	0.00	11	0.86
New Brunswick	0	0.00	22	1.76	71	5.57
Quebec	2	0.42	1	0.08	6	0.47
Ontario	24	5.03	65	5.19	96	7.54
Manitoba	422	88.47	1,097	87.55	972	76.30
Saskatchewan	18	3.77	37	2.95	41	3.22
Alberta	0	0.00	19	1.52	19	1.49
British Columbia	11	2.31	12	0.96	22	1.73
Total	477	100	1,253	100	1,274	100

OTHER CLASS BY CATEGORY
(Principal Applicants and Dependants)

	1999		2000		2001	
CATEGORY	#	%	#	%	#	%
Retirees (Principal Applicants)	2	0.05	0	0.00	0	0.00
Retirees (Dependants)	7	0.16	0	0.00	0	0.00
Live-in Caregivers (Principal Applicants)	2,631	61.31	2,279	70.27	2,286	80.83
Live-in Caregivers (Dependants)	629	14.66	504	15.54	337	11.92
DROC* and PDRCC** (Principal Applicants)	559	13.03	260	8.02	108	3.82
DROC* and PDRCC** (Dependants)	463	10.79	200	6.17	97	3.43
Total	4,291	100	3,243	100	2,828	100

* DROC: Deferred Removal Orders Class

** PDRCC: Post-Determination Refugee Claimants in Canada Class

OTHER CLASS BY TOP TEN SOURCE COUNTRIES
(Principal Applicants and Dependants)

COUNTRY	1999 #	%	Rank	2000 #	%	Rank	2001 #	%	Rank
Philippines	2,802	65.30	1	2,383	73.48	1	2,272	80.34	1
Slovak Republic	71	1.65	6	51	1.57	5	65	2.30	2
Sri Lanka	49	1.14	8	56	1.73	4	40	1.41	3
United Kingdom	55	1.28	7	30	0.93	9	29	1.03	4
India	74	1.72	5	58	1.79	2	27	0.95	5
Czech Republic	23	0.54	15	24	0.74	11	26	0.92	6
Pakistan	174	4.06	3	36	1.11	7	20	0.71	7
France	37	0.86	10	39	1.20	6	19	0.67	8
China	287	6.69	2	56	1.73	3	18	0.64	9
Ukraine	11	0.26	24	13	0.40	18	17	0.60	10
Jamaica	30	0.70	12	28	0.86	10	14	0.50	12
Ghana	74	1.72	4	33	1.02	8	9	0.32	18
Bangladesh	41	0.96	9	22	0.68	12	0	0.00	87
Total for Top Ten Only	3,664	85.38		2,770	85.42		2,533		
Total Other Countries	627	14.62		473	14.58		295	10.43	
Total	4,291	100		3,243			2,828	100	

New Immigrants 2001 & 2002 Comparison

Immigration levels came well within the 2002 Immigration Plan's range of 210,000 to 235,000 new immigrants. A total of 228,575 new immigrants came to Canada in 2002. This figure represented a decline of nine percent compared to 2001, or almost 22,000 fewer immigrants. Higher levels were achieved in 2001 through the federal budget provision of special funds to reduce the inventory of immigrant applications at missions overseas.

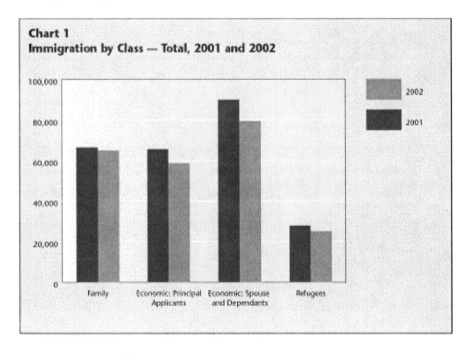

Chart 1
Immigration by Class — Total, 2001 and 2002

Countries of Origin

For the fifth year running, China was the leading source country of immigrants to Canada, accounting for just over 33,000 new immigrants in 2002, or 15 percent of the year's total. China's landings declined by 18 percent compared to 2001--a relatively larger drop than the decline in overall immigrant numbers.

The second and third largest source countries (India and Pakistan, respectively) experienced less dramatic change over 2001 figures. India continued to send a growing number of immigrants to Canada in 2002, rising three percent for the year to 28,754. Pakistan's numbers declined by eight percent compared to 2001. Overall, India provided 13 percent of immigrants to Canada in 2002, while Pakistan sent six percent of the total.

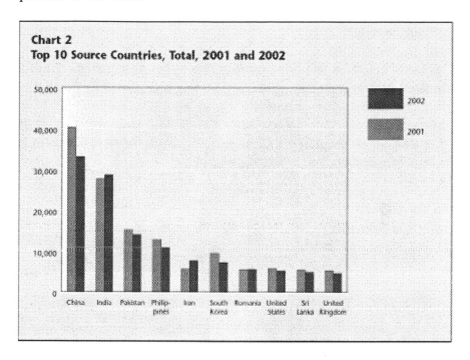

Chart 2
Top 10 Source Countries, Total, 2001 and 2002

Landing Categories

Economic immigrants accounted for 60 percent of landings in 2002 (138,226 principal applicants and dependants), while the family class accounted for 29 percent (65,087) and refugees for 11 percent (25,098). The percentage of landings in each category did not change significantly from 2001.

Taking a look at principal applicant numbers, skilled worker landings decreased by nine percent, a figure that matched the drop in the overall immigrant levels in 2002. The number of business immigrants continued to decline through 2002 to a year-end drop of 26 percent. Live-in caregiver landings also declined by about 24 percent compared to 2001.

Landings in the provincial nominee category grew by 65 percent in 2002 (679 principal applicants). The increases reflected a number of new and expanded provincial nominee agreements signed between the federal government and several provinces, including Manitoba, P.E.I., Alberta and Nova Scotia, among others.

Destinations

Some 49 percent of 2002 immigrants were destined to Toronto on arrival in Canada--a proportion that has been roughly maintained in the past three years. Another 14 percent were destined for Montréal and 13 percent for Vancouver. Vancouver has seen its share of Canada's new immigrants drop steadily since 1999, when it received about 17 percent of new immigrants.

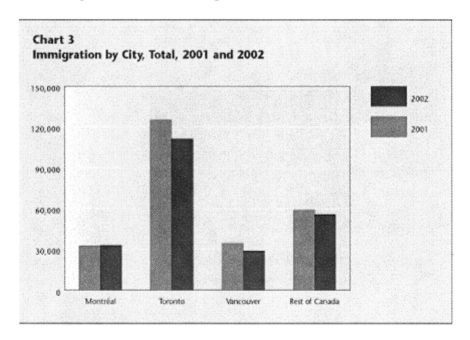

Chart 3
Immigration by City, Total, 2001 and 2002

Skill Levels

Notable declines occurred at skill level A (professionals), whose 2002 total reflected a drop of 21 percent (almost 6,700 fewer workers) over the previous year. The decline was especially sharp in the last two quarters of the year; the final quarter figures declined 37 percent compared to the fourth quarter of 2001. Part of this decline can be attributed to a regulatory change under IRPA. For example, performing artist groups of fewer than 15 people no longer require work permits. Only 2,020 artists entered under the category in 2002, and all in the first six months of the year. This compares to about 5,500 in 2001--35 percent of who were from the U.S. Similar declines were recorded at skill level B (skilled and technical workers), with year-end totals down by 12 percent (around 1,750 fewer workers) compared to 2001, and a decline of 36 percent in the final quarter. IRPA regulations extended the after-sales servicing provisions under NAFTA to people of all countries of origin. Prior to the regulatory change, about 5,000 people a year was issued work permits for after-sales servicing, about 60 percent of whom were classified at skill level B.

Workers at skill level C (intermediate and clerical, including seasonal agricultural workers) gained three percent in 2002, becoming the largest single group of foreign workers in Canada. Flows reached 26,455 workers for the year. Despite the overall rise, the fourth quarter reflected a modest decline over the same period in 2001, dropping by three percent.

Workers at the lowest skill level (D - elemental and labour) declined by five percent over 2001 totals, but accounted for only one percent of overall foreign worker flows.

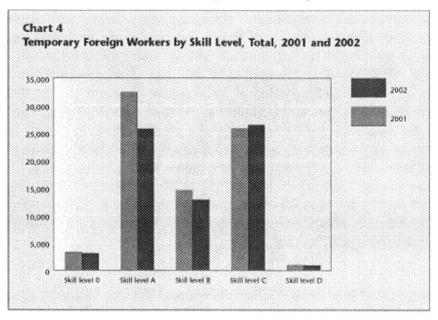

Chart 4
Temporary Foreign Workers by Skill Level, Total, 2001 and 2002

Destinations

British Columbia and the provinces of Atlantic Canada (except New Brunswick) increased their numbers of foreign workers in 2002, ranging from eight percent growth in British Columbia to 11 percent for P.E.I. This added almost 1,200 more workers to British Columbia, with Nova Scotia adding the next largest group with almost 200 more.

Among Canada's largest cities, only Vancouver increased the number of foreign workers, adding 10 percent compared to 2001. Montréal and Toronto's numbers dropped 15 and seven percent, respectively. Among Canada's smaller cities, several recorded substantial drops, including Ottawa, down 24 percent (700 fewer workers); Edmonton, down 23 percent (almost 500 fewer workers); and Winnipeg, down 24 percent (almost 300 fewer workers). These declines are partly attributable to the new IRPA regulations

CHAPTER - II

WELCOME TO CANADA

WHAT YOU SHOULD KNOW

Table of Contents

WELCOME TO CANADA!

*C*ongratulations! You have taken a big step. Moving to a new country takes courage. It also creates exciting opportunities and new beginnings. Taking the time to learn what to expect -- and what is expected of you -- will help you succeed. This guide tells you a little about what it's like to live in Canada. It also lets you know who can help if you need more information. We hope it will help you adapt to your new life. Be assured that those who already live in Canada add their wishes for your happiness and success in your new country.

Your first year in Canada will be emotional and full of change. You may be looking for a place to live, a job, and schools for your children. You will probably make many new friends. Some of them will know how it feels to move to a new community or new country.

Regardless of your situation, being a newcomer may mean giving up some familiar things for a new way of life. As a result, you may feel anxious or afraid, especially during the first few days and weeks. Almost all newcomers experience these emotions as they settle in. Feeling at home in a new country takes time.

The best way to adjust to your new community is to become involved! Do not hesitate to speak English or French, even if you make mistakes. Understanding and speaking one of Canada's official languages will help you adapt more easily. As you talk with the people you meet, you will feel more in control of your new life. Use each day as an opportunity to learn. Ask questions whenever you need to. Most people are pleased to help. Canadians believe in the spirit of community. No matter which city or town you choose to live in, you will find people who can help you adapt to your new life, and fit into Canadian society.

In the weeks, months and years ahead, you will have many opportunities to participate fully in Canadian life. Take them. You and your family can grow together, side by side with other Canadians, and make a better life for everyone. This is your new home. Welcome to Canada!

Sources of information

- **How to find information**
- **Getting around**
- **Using the telephone**
- **The telephone book**
- **Call centres and touch-tone telephones**
- **Emergency 911**
- **Voice mail**
- **Pay phones**
- **Directory assistance**
- **Toll-free numbers**
- **Telephone services for people with special needs**
- **Using computers**
- **Public libraries**

How to find information

*T*he Government of Canada has designed this guide for you -- the new resident in Canada. It includes some basic information about living in Canada. The guide also contains many telephone numbers and addresses, which should be helpful in the next few days, and during the next few years. It can refer you to the help you need, or tell you how to find it.

You may have already received general information about your new country. But what you'll need to know now is more specific. Where can you take language classes? What about housing? How do you go about finding a job in Canada? Whom do you call to find out about schools for your children?

The *Welcome to Canada* guidebook and pamphlets can help you find the answers to these questions. Canada is a huge country, and every province is different. While we can't provide you with all the information you need, we may be able to refer you to the departments, agencies, and organizations, which can help you. Some may be able to help you directly; others may refer you to another source of information.

Immigrant-serving organizations can help you to settle into Canadian society, and many of their services are free. Contact an immigrant-serving organization to find what services are provided. You may find the addresses and telephone numbers of some of these organizations in the pamphlet called *Finding Help in Your Community*, which is in the back pocket of this guide. Many of these organizations represent a number of different immigrant services and groups, so they are a great place to start.

Canada's three levels of government -- federal, provincial and municipal -- also offer a variety of helpful programs and services for newcomers. Who offers these programs and services may vary across Canada, since different provinces have different immigration agreements with the federal government. You will find commonly used government telephone numbers listed in the pamphlet called *Key Information Sources*, which is in the back pocket of this guide. To find out about free language training in your area, please refer to the pamphlet called *Language Training*, also in the back pocket of this guide.

Since the province of Quebec looks after many important aspects of its immigration program, this guide does not attempt to cover services in this province. If you are planning to move to Quebec, you may wish to pick up their guide for newcomers, entitled: *Vivre au QUÉBEC!* You can obtain this booklet from the *ministère des Relations avec les citoyens et de l'Immigration (MRCI)*. You will find the MRCI telephone numbers for your area listed in the pamphlets called *Key Information Sources* and *Finding Help in Your Community*, which are in the back pocket of this guide.

Religious institutions, community groups, ethnic associations and newcomer clubs, which can give you a hand are probably located right in your neighbourhood. Their telephone numbers can be found in the local telephone book.

Remember, the information and services provided may vary from one place to another. To get the most out of this guide and the pamphlets that go with it, we suggest that you:

- get a map of your community;
- get a copy of the local telephone book; and

- contact the immigrant-serving organizations in your community.

This guide, along with an immigrant-serving organization, can help you through the steps you need to take to settle. It can help you sort out the information you are missing and what services you need. The *Welcome to Canada* guide also includes a checklist to help you with the things you need to do first.

Getting around

It is useful to have a map of the area where you will be living. It will help you to get around and find the services you need. Most bookstores, gas stations and convenience stores sell maps at a reasonable price. You may also be able to get a map of your community free through your local Chamber of Commerce or municipal office. You can also look at maps in the library, at no cost. However, you can't take maps out of the library.

Using the telephone

Canadians like to use the telephone for communicating. They talk on the telephone everywhere -- at home, in their cars, on the street, in telephone booths. You will find that telephone books are great sources of information. Most of the important telephone numbers you need can be found in alphabetical order in the telephone book. You will receive one from the company, which installs a telephone in your home. You may also be able to pick one up from a phone centre. Phone centres are often located in large shopping malls. There are also telephone books at the library, and where you find pay phones.

At home: You pay a basic rate each month for telephone service. This pays for all local calls. You will be charged extra for each long distance call you make. Long distance calls are made to telephone numbers outside your local area.

Away from home: Pay phones in most provinces cost 25 cents per local call, and you can find them in most public places. If you do not know a telephone number, dial 411 and ask the operator. There is a charge for using this number. You may also purchase telephone cards, which can be used to call anywhere from any telephone, including public telephones.

The telephone book

Telephone books in Canada include white, blue, and yellow pages. The white pages list home telephone numbers in and around your area, as well as some businesses. The blue pages list government numbers. The yellow pages list business numbers -- restaurants, services, stores, and so on. These are listed by subject or product.

In the front part of the telephone book you will find emergency numbers like fire departments and ambulance services. The most important number listed here is an emergency number, 911 in many provinces, which you can call for help in life-threatening emergencies.

The white pages of the telephone book list home and business numbers in alphabetical order, from A to Z, using the last name of the person listed. So look up John Smith under S, for Smith.

The blue pages of the telephone book list telephone numbers for Canadian government departments, including the federal, provincial, municipal and regional governments. For frequently used government telephone numbers, see the pamphlet called *Key Information Sources,* in the back pocket of this guide.

The yellow pages are found in a separate telephone book in some of the larger cities in Canada.

Call centres and touch-tone telephones

Many businesses and government departments receive so many calls that they have set up "call centres" to help them answer the most commonly asked questions. Call centres use a series of messages, which have already been recorded to answer your questions. You find these messages by using the numbers, letters and symbols on the keys of your touch-tone telephone. The call centre message will tell you which keys on your telephone to press for the information you need. If you miss it the first time around, the message will usually tell you which key to press to hear it again. The list of messages is usually called a "menu." You choose and order the information you want.

You can also enter information into some call centres, using the keys on the telephone.

Remember: the "pound" key is the one that looks like this [#]. The "star" key looks like this [*].

Emergency 911

If you fear for your safety, or the safety of someone in your family, you should call your local emergency number for help. In many Canadian cities this number is 911. This connects you immediately to ambulances, fire departments, the police, and other emergency services. In other communities not equipped with 911 services, dial 0 and ask the operator for help. Other medical emergency numbers are listed in the first few white pages of the telephone book. These may include a poison information number, a distress or sexual assault help line, and a number to call if you or someone in your family is being abused.

Voice mail

Many Canadians, and most Canadian businesses and departments, have some form of answering machine or service to take messages for them when they are away from their phones. The telephone may ring several times, and then a recorded message will ask you to leave your name and number and a short message. You will usually hear a beeping sound followed by a silence. At this point leave your spoken message and remember to speak clearly and slowly. You may want to repeat your telephone number twice.

Pay phones

You may want to use a public telephone when you are out, or before you get your telephone installed. There are many pay telephone booths set up on city streets, in shopping malls, in airports -- anywhere there are lots of people. You pay for these telephone calls as you use the telephone. For local calls, you put in 25 cents (this charge may vary in some provinces) and make your call. You should have the right number of coins to put in the slot. If the call is long distance, you will need to put in more money (coins) as you go along, and an operator, or the message across the screen on the pay telephone, will tell you how much. Make sure you have lots of coins with you! Eventually, you may want to get a calling card from a telephone company. This card allows you to dial in a special code and make calls on public phones without putting in any money. These calls are then billed on your regular telephone bill at home.

Directory assistance

If you need help finding a telephone number, you may call for assistance. Call 411 for local numbers, and 0 for overseas numbers. All telephone numbers have an area code, which refers to the location of the number. You can look up these codes in your local telephone book. If the call you wish to make is outside the local area code, it is probably going to be long distance. *Call 1+AREA CODE+555-1212* if you need help to find the number. Remember, there is a charge for using this service.

Toll-free numbers

Canada is a very large country, and it can be expensive to make calls from one city to another. Many businesses and government departments use telephone numbers that start with **1-800, 1-888, or 1-877**. This lets you call them for free, within a province, or within Canada. These are known as toll-free numbers. Simply dial the 1-800, 1-888, or 1-877 number exactly as listed.

Telephone services for people with special needs

Many telephone companies in Canada can provide special telephone equipment for people with a hearing, speech, visual or physical disability. Contact your local telephone company to get more information on these kinds of services and equipment. You can find the name of the telephone company in your area by looking at a telephone book in a pay telephone. The Customer Service number is usually in the first few pages of the book. In areas served by Bell Canada, you can also visit a Bell Phone centre. These are usually found in large shopping malls.

Using computers

A great deal of helpful information is now available through the Internet, a worldwide resource and information system. You don't need to own a computer or have Internet access at home to use it. You can often use the Internet (or "surf the web," as Canadians like to say), free of charge at your local public library (you must reserve a time slot), community centre, school, immigrant-serving organization or Human Resources Development Canada office. Useful information can be found on various "web sites," which are like codes or addresses on the Internet.

Public libraries

In most communities across Canada, there are public libraries which can be used free of charge. Libraries are a resource which many newcomers make use of to read the daily newspapers, use the internet and borrow books.

☑ **Do you have a map of the area where you will be living?**
☑ **Do you know how to use a telephone book?**

GETTING TO KNOW CANADA

- **The Canadian way of life**

The Canadian way of life

*C*anada is an immense country. It is very diverse in its people, its landscape, its climate and its way of life. However, Canadians do share the same important values. These values guide and influence much of our everyday life. These are values of pride, a belief in equality and diversity and respect for all individuals in society. Women, men, children and seniors are all equally respected in Canada. Canadians may be different from each other but it is these shared values that make Canada a friendly, caring, peace loving and secure society in which to live.

Fairness, tolerance and respect. Canadians want fairness and justice for themselves, their children and their families. And most are fair and just to others, no matter who they are or where they come from.

Diversity and cooperation. Canadians understand the value of cooperation. In a country as large and diverse as Canada, people must be able to learn to resolve or ignore small conflicts in order to live happily and peacefully.

Equal opportunity. Canadians believe in equality. Each person is equal before the law and is treated equally by the law. Women and men have the same opportunity for success. Canadians let people live as they wish, as long as they do not limit how others live.

Civil responsibility. Canadians appreciate their rights and freedoms, which are the same without regard to gender, race, or ethnicity. Most also want to contribute to our society. As a newcomer, you should be aware of your rights and responsibilities. The right to participate in Canadian society implies an obligation to help it succeed. Canadian citizenship is about caring enough to want to get involved and make Canada even better.

Environmental responsibility. Canadians are especially conscious of their natural environment and the need to both respect and protect it for the future. For example, individual Canadians participate in recycling programs that help convert "garbage" into usable materials. Canadians also like to keep their parks and streets clean, by putting their garbage into garbage cans and cleaning up after their pets. In many public places, smoking is not permitted.

BASIC SERVICES

- **Citizenship and Immigration Canada (CIC) Call Centres**
- **Immigrant-serving organizations**
- **Host Program**
- **Immigrant Settlement and Adaptation Program (ISAP)**
- **LINC (Language Instruction for Newcomers)**
- **Government services**

Citizenship and Immigration Canada (CIC) Call Centres

*Y*ou can get general information about immigration and citizenship by calling the CIC Call Centre. Recorded information is available 24 hours a day, seven days a week, in English or French. If you have access to the Internet, you can also view the CIC Web site (http://www.cic.gc.ca) for recent announcements, publications, and application kits and guides. (See the section on "Using computers" for further information on Internet web sites.)

The CIC Call Centre can provide:

- general information about immigration and citizenship programs and services;
- general information about your application;
- application and information kits;
- help with fee calculations.

Remember: If you have an immigration client identification (ID) number, you will need it to obtain information about your application.

Here's how it works:

1. A recorded message will tell you to press 1 or 2 to select English or French.
2. The recorded message will list a "menu" from which to choose the information you need. Press the star [*] key to repeat the message.
3. Press 9 to return to the main menu and make your choice.
4. During normal business hours (8 a.m. to 4 p.m.) across Canada, you can press 0 to speak directly to a program

assistant. If all the assistants are busy, stay on the line until one becomes free.

How to contact the Call Centre:

If you are in the local calling area of:

Montreal, call: **514-496-1010**

Toronto, call: **416-973-4444**

Vancouver, call: **604-666-2171**

If you are anywhere else in Canada, call toll-free: 1-888-242-2100. If you wish to use the Internet, the address is http://www.cic.gc.ca.

Remember: One of the most frequent reasons for calling the Call Centre is to obtain application kits for Citizenship and Immigration services. These include sponsorship or citizenship applications. You don't need to speak to an assistant to order these kits -- simply follow the recorded instructions and leave your name and mailing address, including the postal code.

Immigrant-serving organizations

Canada has hundreds of organizations, which help newcomers settle into life in Canada. Many of them represent a number of different multicultural agencies and associations, so they can help you in several ways. They may provide language training, or help you find housing, or look for a job. They may also provide support for women, children, and families who are dealing with domestic violence. Some of these organizations can provide these services in your first language, which may be helpful in the first few months. The addresses and telephone numbers of many of these organizations are listed in the pamphlet *Finding Help in Your Community*, found in the back pocket of this brochure.

Host Program

The Host program is a federal government program, designed to:

- Match you with a friend familiar with Canadian ways,
- Help you overcome the stress of moving to a new country,
- Help you learn about available services and how to use them,

- Help you practice English or French,
- Help you develop contacts in your employment field,
- And help you participate in community activities.

In return, the host volunteer will have you as a new friend, learn about your culture and strengthen community life.

Immigrant Settlement and Adaptation Program (ISAP)

ISAP is a federal government program, designed to:

- Help you with immediate needs,
- Refer you to economic, social, health, cultural, educational and recreational facilities,
- Provide you with information and orientation on banking, shopping, managing a household and so on,
- Provide you with interpretation or translation services when necessary,
- Provide you with short-term counseling,
- And provide you with employment-related services.

LINC (Language Instruction for Newcomers)

LINC is a federal government program for adults that is designed to:

- Assess your level of English or French through the LINC Assessment Centres,
- Refer you to an appropriate LINC Provider through the Assessment Centres,
- Provide you, through School boards, Colleges and Community Organizations, with full-time, part-time, evening, weekend and other classes based on your needs,
- Provide you with transportation and child minding when necessary.

Government services

The main telephone numbers for federal, provincial, and municipal or regional government departments are listed in the blue pages of your local telephone book. Some are listed by department, or by service. Frequently called numbers are often listed at the beginning of each section, including a central information number.

If you need help to find a federal government program or service, call Information on the Government of Canada at 1-800-622-6232 or if you wish to use the Internet, the address is:

If you wish to use the Internet, the address is:
http://www.canada.gc.ca

WHERE TO BEGIN

- **Papers and other identity documents**
- **Using public transportation**
- **Where to stay**
- **Canadian money**
- **Shopping**
- **Going out of town**

Papers and other identity documents

*O*fficial papers, which relate to who you are and where you come from are extremely important. They can be hard to replace if you lose them. These include health records, birth certificates, and Records of Landing (IMM 1000). If you are living in Quebec, you will have a *Certificat de selection du Québec* (CSQ). You will need these papers to apply for important government services and benefits, and to obtain a Social Insurance Number card and Health Insurance Card. So it is very important to keep them in a safe place at all times, and not to lend them to your friends or let someone else use them. You could lose your benefits if you give your cards to someone else.

It is not necessary to carry your passport or visa around with you, but it is important to have a couple of pieces of ID (identification) with you at all times. Any two of the following would be good: a driver's licence, a photocopy of your permanent resident papers (the original should be kept in a safe place or in a safety deposit box at the bank), a Social Insurance Number card, a Health Insurance Card, and a credit card.

Using public transportation

Getting around in Canada is fairly easy. Most cities have urban transportation systems, including buses, streetcars, and trains, and some of the larger cities also have subways.

You can board these systems at regular stops along their routes. Some let you pay with cash; others require tickets. If you don't have a ticket for the bus, you must pay with the right amount of money (exact fare).

This is because the driver does not carry any change. Once you get settled, you may want to buy a monthly pass or a package of tickets to save money. You can buy subway tickets at the subway station.

If you have to take several buses or the subway for a single trip, you do not need to pay each time. Simply ask the driver for a transfer, or pick one up from the machines on the subway platform.

If you are not sure where to board the bus or the streetcar, just ask someone, or follow the crowd. It's usually at the front of the bus, where you show your pass to the driver. When using public transportation, Canadians line up. First come, first served, is a common approach to many activities in Canada.

Maps of routes and schedules are usually available from the public transit company in your area, and there may also be a telephone information line. You may want to ask someone for the name of the transit company where you live, and then look it up in the white pages of your telephone book.

Where to stay

For the first few weeks or months, you will probably want to find some temporary housing while you look for a more permanent place to live. Hotels can be quite expensive, so you may want to rent a furnished room or apartment at first.

To help you in your search, you could check the classified ads in the daily newspaper in your area. Look under Apartments or Houses for Rent. You should also talk to the immigrant-serving organizations in your community. They might be able to help.

Canadian money

Canada's currency is the dollar. There are 100 cents in a dollar. Canadian coins include the penny (1 cent), nickel (5 cents), dime (10 cents), quarter (25 cents), a one-dollar coin known as the "loonie," and a two-dollar coin called a "toonie". The most common paper bills are $5, $10, $20 and $50.

Chances are that when you get to Canada you will have some Canadian money with you. If you don't, you may wish to exchange a small amount of your native currency for some Canadian money as soon as you arrive. Most airports have foreign exchange offices, which can do this for you. Try not to exchange too much, however, since the rate of exchange (how much your money will buy) may not be as good as at a local bank.

Shopping

In the first few days you may need a few supplies, like food and extra clothing. Stores in Canada may be set up a little differently than what you have experienced in other countries.

Most Canadian stores have central cashiers where you pay for your goods, but they can be hard to find. Grocery stores usually have rows of cashiers at the entrance to the store, and you bring your goods to the cash, line up and pay. Department stores, which sell a variety of products, are sometimes set up this way too. Other stores have cashiers set up in different places around the store, and you pay at the nearest cashier. You will receive a paper receipt for whatever you buy, and this is your "proof of payment."

Many stores in Canada have metal shopping carts where you can put your purchases as you make your way through the store to the cashier.

Many Canadian stores are grouped together in large shopping malls, so you can do all your shopping in one place. Remember that each store has its own cash register where you pay for your purchases.

Many places in Canada also have large open-air markets, where you can buy fresh fruits and vegetables from local farmers. You pay for your purchases as you go along, from the farmers at each "stand."

Going out of town

Buses, trains and planes travel throughout Canada. For out-of-town trips, contact travel agencies, airline companies or bus lines. For information about train travel, contact Via Rail. The telephone numbers are listed in the yellow pages.

☑ **Have you got any Canadian money?**

☑ **Are your identity papers in a safe place?**

☑ **Do you have some form of identification with you?**

HEALTH SERVICES

- **Applying for a Health Insurance Card**
- **Finding doctors and clinics**
- **Emergency help**
- **Immunization for children**
- **Immunization for adults**
- **Medical surveillance**
- **Pregnancy**
- **To find out more...**

Applying for a Health Insurance Card

*C*anada has one of the finest health insurance programs in the world. Health insurance means that you don't have to "pay" directly for most health care services. They are paid for through your taxes. When you use these services, you simply present your Health Insurance Card.

While health insurance is a national service, each province administers its own program. There may be some variations for eligibility from province to province. In some provinces you will have to pay a small monthly fee for this insurance. It is important to apply for your Health Insurance Card as soon as possible. You will receive your Health Insurance Card from the province where you live. You can get an application form at a doctor's office, a hospital, a pharmacy or an immigrant-serving organization. You can also get forms from the provincial ministry responsible for health, listed in the blue pages of your telephone book. You will need to show some identification, such as your birth certificate or passport and/or Record of Landing (IMM 1000).

Permanent residents in British Columbia, Ontario, Quebec and New Brunswick have a three-month eligibility-waiting period. During this time, you should apply for temporary private, health insurance coverage. Private insurance companies are listed in the yellow pages of the telephone book, usually under "Insurance." Private health insurance is also available for services, which are not covered under the government health insurance plan. These might include dental costs or private hospital rooms. Some employers also offer additional health insurance for a monthly deduction from your pay cheque. In most provinces, health insurance does not cover the cost of prescription drugs, dental care, ambulance services and prescription eyeglasses.

Needy refugee claimants and refugees living in the provinces, which have the three-month eligibility-waiting period, can receive emergency and essential health services. The cost of these services is covered by the Interim Federal Health Program.

Remember: Each member of your family needs his or her own Health Insurance Card. Always bring your card with you when you go to the doctor or the hospital.

A Health Insurance Card must not be exchanged with anyone else. It is for your use only and you could lose the benefits it provides by letting other people use it. You could also face criminal charges and be removed from Canada.

Finding doctors and clinics

Most Canadians have a family doctor and dentist. Ask an immigrant service organization or someone you know to recommend one. You can also look them up in the yellow pages of the telephone book under "Physicians and Surgeons," or "Dentists." Canada also has a large number of medical clinics, which can offer a variety of health services without an appointment, or in a minor emergency. These are listed under "Clinics" or "Clinics-Medical" in the yellow pages.

Emergency help

If you need urgent medical help, quickly go to the emergency department of your nearest hospital or call the emergency number "911."

If you have a serious medical condition, such as diabetes, high blood pressure or allergies to medications, ask your doctor or hospital about Medic Alert tags and bracelets. These can provide useful information in an emergency.

Immunization for children

Immunization or vaccination for children is one of the most effective ways we protect all Canadians, young and old, from getting serious infectious diseases. These diseases include diphtheria, polio and tetanus. Your child gets a small dose of vaccine to help him or her build up "immunity" to these diseases. You can arrange to have your child inoculated through your doctor or pediatrician, or through a public health clinic. You will receive an immunization or vaccination record, which you may have to provide to your child's school.

In Canada there is a "schedule" for these immunizations. For example, some shots are given when your child is two months old, at four months, at six months, and so on. Ask your doctor or pediatrician for a copy of this schedule, or look up the municipal department responsible for school immunization in the blue pages of your telephone book. You may also find a central help line listed under "Immunization" in the white pages of the telephone book. The schedule varies slightly from province to province.

Immunization for adults

If you were not immunized against preventable diseases before coming to Canada, you should contact your doctor or local public health clinic immediately.

Medical surveillance

During the medical exam you underwent before becoming a Canadian resident, you may have been told that you needed a follow-up medical exam once you got to Canada. This is known as medical surveillance for those who have an inactive infectious disease. You must report, by telephone, to the public health authority of the province or territory where you live within 30 days of entering Canada. You will find this number in the blue pages of your telephone book. This is very important for your health, and for the health of your fellow Canadians.

Pregnancy

Maternity leave is the right of all working mothers in Canada. If you are pregnant and have to stop working for a while, you can take leave, from your employer for a set period of time. You may also be entitled to paid leave, or maternity benefits. You can get more information from the provincial ministry responsible for labour or from a Human Resources Development Canada office.

For help and information before and after your baby is born, contact your local community service centre or hospital. They offer prenatal courses, medical help, nursing care, and a way to meet other new mothers. They can also give you information on registering the birth with the province, so that you receive an official birth certificate. They can also advise you about birth control and abortion.

☑ **Have you applied for your Health Insurance Card?**

To find out more...

Key medical emergency numbers are listed in the front section of the white pages of your telephone book. Look up doctors and clinics in the yellow pages. There is also printed health information available from provincial ministries of health and from Citizenship and Immigration Canada. Free pamphlets are also available on a variety of topics from Health Canada (found in the federal listings in the blue pages of your telephone book), or from doctor's offices and drug stores.

ESTABLISHING YOURSELF

- **Applying for a Social Insurance Number card**
- **Applying for the Canada Child Tax Benefit**

Applying for a Social Insurance Number card

pplying for a Social Insurance Number (SIN) card is one of the most important things you will do after coming to Canada. You will need one to work here, to open a bank account or to obtain your tax credit. This number tells the government who is earning money, paying taxes, paying into pension plans, and using government services. Your employers will ask you for this number.

To apply for one, simply go to your nearest Human Resources Development Canada office (listed in the blue pages of your telephone book). As a new immigrant, you will need to provide the original of your Record of Landing (IMM 1000). If the name you are using to apply for your SIN card is different than the one found on the document you are providing, you must also provide either a marriage certificate or a change of name document.

Remember: You must make sure that the name on all documents is the same name. This name must always belong to the same person, and it must be spelled correctly.

Applying for the Canada Child Tax Benefit

If you have children under 18, the Government of Canada may be able to help you with some of the costs of raising them. This monthly tax-free payment is called the Canada Child Tax Benefit. The amount of the benefit is based on several factors, such as: your family income, the number of children you have and their ages, and your province or territory of residence. When you apply, you must provide proof of your Canadian immigration status, and proof of birth for any of your children born outside of Canada.

To apply for the Canada Child Tax Benefit, you must have filed an Income Tax and Benefit Return. If you were not residents of Canada in time to fill out a return, you will need to complete a separate form to declare your world income. You can get these forms and more information on the Canada Child Tax Benefit by calling the Canada Customs and Revenue Agency at (613) 941-9300 or the toll-free number: 1-800-387-1193, or visit http://www.ccra-adrc.gc.ca

If you live in Quebec, Canada Customs and Revenue Agency will automatically send the Régie des rentes du Québec all information needed to register your children for the Quebec family allowance.

FINDING A PLACE TO LIVE

- **Renting**
- **Your rights as a tenant**
- **Buying**
- **Heat and hydro**
- **Getting a telephone**
- **Furnishing**
- **To find out more...**

Renting

*M*any Canadians rent housing, and so do most newcomers, at least for the first few years. Apartments and houses for rent are usually listed in the classified advertising section of the newspaper. It is also a good idea to walk around an area you would like to live in, and see if there are any signs posted on or by the buildings. Do not take the first place you see -- try to shop around a little, see what's available. Prices often vary considerably.

Some apartments can be rented by the month, but with most rented housing you sign a lease for a year. This is a legally binding contract between you and the landlord. Make sure you understand exactly what you have to pay for, and what is included in your rent. For example, do you pay for the heating costs or are they included? Canada is a cold country in the winter, and heating can be expensive. Are you allowed to have pets? Are the fridge and stove included? Do you have to pay municipal taxes? Also, you may have to pay a security deposit (such as the first month's rent) to rent the apartment you have chosen. Read the lease over carefully before you sign it.

You should also purchase tenant's insurance to cover the costs of replacing the household contents of your apartment. It is probably a good idea to ask someone in your local community group or immigrant-serving organization for information about housing. They can also explain the legal terms used in leases.

Remember: Avoid signing a lease if you plan to move again soon.

Your rights as a tenant

Both tenants (someone who rents a room, an apartment or house) and landlords both have legal rights. There are laws, which protect you from sudden rent increases or being forced to leave your apartment. You have the right to live anywhere you choose. Discrimination on the basis of colour, creed, sex, age or disability is not allowed by the *Canadian Charter of Rights and Freedoms.* Provincial landlord and tenant laws also protect against such discrimination. You also have responsibilities. It is important to keep the house or apartment you are renting in the same condition you found it. Call the provincial or municipal government department responsible for housing, sometimes called a rental board, if you need information or help, or look up the provincial Landlord and Tenant Regulations. You will find the numbers in the blue pages of the telephone book. You can also ask community groups for information or help.

Buying

Buying a home is a big step, and you might want to wait until you are settled before you do so. Most homes in Canada are sold through real estate agents, although some owners do it themselves. You may see "For Sale" signs posted in front of homes, and you can also read the classified advertising section of the daily newspaper.

When buying a house, it's important to remember that there are many hidden costs. These may include the agent's fee, in some provinces, as well as lawyer's or notary's fees, yearly property tax, house insurance, registration fees, various home buyer taxes, and the cost of maintaining the house -- heat, hydro, water, sewer, and so on. Make sure you know exactly what your costs will be before you buy.

You may want to find out about the First Home Loan Insurance Program, run by Canada Mortgage and Housing Corporation. It enables you to buy a home with a smaller down payment. The Corporation's fee is rolled into the total mortgage in the form of a small percentage.

Heat and hydro

Whether you rent or buy, you will need to sign up for various basic services, such as heat and hydro (electricity). In Canada, some homes are heated by gas, others by oil, and others by electricity. Frequently, there are one or two main companies, which provide these services in an area, and you can find these in the yellow pages of the telephone book. Try looking under "Gas," "Heating Companies," "Oils/Fuel," and "Hydro-Electric."

Getting a telephone

You will want to get a telephone installed quickly, so that you can reach the people and the services you need from the comfort of your home. Bell Canada operates most of the telephone service across Canada, but you can find out the name of the telephone company in your area in a telephone book. The Customer Service number should be in the first few pages of the book. The telephone company in your area normally has phone centres in large shopping malls. You can visit them to get your service set up.

You can either rent a telephone from your telephone company and pay month by month or buy one. The cost of making local calls is covered by the monthly service fee, which is added to the cost of renting the telephone. Long distance and overseas calls are not covered by this monthly fee, and can be quite expensive. Many telephone companies offer special plans, which can reduce the costs of long distance calls. Phone cards, which can be used to call anywhere from any phone including public telephones, are a cost-effective way to reduce long-distance charges.

Remember: Canada is a very large country, so even when you're calling within the same province or city, long distance charges may apply.

Furnishing

Chances are you're going to need some basic furniture and household appliances. You can buy new, which can be costly, or wait for stores to have sales and buy things gradually. You can also buy used furniture and appliances, which is what many Canadians do. Articles or furniture for sale listings are found in the classified advertising section of the newspaper. You can also try used furniture stores, church and local rummage or garage sales, or community organizations. Your local community immigrant service organization should be able to help you with names and addresses.

To find out more...

Probably one of the best sources of information is your local immigrant-serving organization. You might also want to consult the provincial or municipal department responsible for housing, listed in the blue pages of your telephone book. They may have a central information number.

The Canada Mortgage and Housing Corporation (CMHC) has a free pamphlet entitled *Home buying, Step by Step.* They also run the Canada Housing Information Centre, and can provide information on the rental and housing markets across Canada. Call their toll-free number for more information: 1-800-668-2642 or visit their website at http://www.cmhc-schl.gc.ca

☑ Have you contacted your telephone company?

☑ Do you have your address and telephone number with you?

☑ Do you know how to get heat and light?

PROTECTING YOUR MONEY

- **Banks and other financial institutions**
- **Opening an account**
- **Using banking machines**
- **Direct deposit**
- **Sending money**
- **Applying for credit**
- **Telemarketing**
- **To find out more...**

Banks and other financial institutions

*M*ost Canadians keep their money in the bank. A bank account is a safe place to keep your money. Banks let you write cheques, earn interest, apply for credit, and pay your bills. These kinds of financial services are also offered by credit unions, caisses populaires and trust companies.

Opening an account

Most banks have various kinds of accounts, and you can discuss which kind you need with them. To open one, you should be prepared to provide certain kinds of personal information, as well as various forms of identification, such as your passport, or your Social Insurance Number. The bank will need your Social Insurance Number for income tax purposes. This is the same for anyone, at any bank. If you have not received your SIN card when you go to open your account, you should present proof that you have applied for one.

Remember: Post Office savings accounts do not exist in Canada.

Using banking machines

Many Canadians now use Automated Banking Machines, known as ATMs, to do most of their banking. It's like a self-service bank, one that's "open" 24 hours a day, seven days a week. With a bankcard, you can use these machines to get cash from your accounts, to pay bills, to deposit cheques, and so on. You will likely pay a small fee for this service.

You can apply for a card at your bank. You will need to create a Personal Identification Number (PIN) for yourself to access your accounts. Don't lend your bankcard to anyone, or tell anyone your PIN. Don't even let anyone see your PIN number when you enter it in the banking machine. This will keep your account (and your money) safe.

Bankcards can also be used to buy things at many stores. The money is taken directly from your account when you use your card. This is known as Interac Direct Payment.

While all of these services are useful, keeping track of all your bank transactions can get complicated. Remember to record everything and take note of your balance and the fees charged by your financial institution.

Direct deposit

Direct deposit has become very popular with Canadians. It means that money owed to you, such as a paycheque or a government payment, is put electronically into your account. You have access to the money immediately, and you don't have to wait for the cheque to come in the mail or line up at the bank to deposit it. You can request this service if you expect to receive regular payments. Most government departments offer this service, as well as many companies.

Sending money

If you send money outside Canada, don't send cash. Use a certified cheque or money order. Ask your bank about these options. You can also buy a money order at the post office or wire money through private money order/transfer services (which are listed in the yellow pages of the telephone book).

Applying for credit

Getting credit means that you borrow money to buy something now and pay it back later, with interest. Interest is the fee charged for using the money. Interest rates can be quite high, so you should be very careful how you use credit.

Credit comes in many forms -- credit cards, lines of credit, mortgages, or loans. You can apply for credit cards at banks and trust companies.

These cards allow you to buy items on credit and be billed for them within a month. If you pay the full amount back by the due date, you won't be charged any interest.

If you borrow any money on credit, make sure you understand exactly when you have to pay it back and how much it will cost. This includes monthly payments if you are borrowing money on an installment plan.

Many department stores now advertise special sales which claim that you can buy something now and pay for it in a year, or in six months with no interest, and so on. Make sure you understand exactly what you must pay and when, before you sign anything. If any information is hard to understand, ask someone you trust for a clear explanation.

Telemarketing

You may get calls from people who are trying to sell you something. They may be honest; but then again, they might be dishonest. The best way to protect yourself is never to give out any personal or financial information to anyone over the telephone. If you feel uneasy about the caller, just hang up.

To find out more...

There is a great deal of free information available to you from your bank, including financial advice. The Canadian Bankers Association also offers a free series of publications, ranging from how to open an account, how to manage your money, how to use bank machines, and how to save for your children's education. You can call their toll-free number to obtain copies: 1-800-263-0231 or you can visit their website at http://www.cba.ca

---

☑ **Have you opened a bank account?**

FINDING A JOB

- **Immigrant-Serving Organizations can help**
- **Human Resources Development Canada offices**
- **Using the newspaper and other resources**
- **Documents and foreign credentials**
- **Getting paid**
- **Working for yourself**
- **Business and travel**
- **Daycare**
- **Labour laws and human rights**
- **Volunteering**

*A*t first you may find it difficult to get work that matches your skills. It may also be difficult to find a job that pays as much as you want until you get Canadian experience. Try not to be discouraged. When the right job does come along, you will have the benefit of that previous experience.

When you apply for a job in Canada, the employer will want some information about you. Bring a list of your education and work experience (a résumé). Also bring letters of reference from your former employers, your professional degrees and trade certificates. You may be asked to provide English or French copies of these documents.

Remember that certain trades or professions are regulated, which means that you must be licensed, registered or certified to practice them. In other words, you must meet certain standards, which are set by the organization responsible for your profession in the province where you plan to work. The standards vary from province to province. So even though you may be qualified in another country, your qualifications must meet Canadian standards for you to be licensed to practice.

Immigrant-Serving Organizations can help

If you cannot speak the language used by the employer, ask a friend to interpret for you, or get a translator through an immigrant-serving organization. You might also want to ask about job finding clubs, about workshops, and about getting help with preparing a résumé or writing a letter. These services are often provided by immigrant-serving organizations themselves or by the province. Refer to the pamphlet *Finding Help in Your Community* in the back pocket of this book.

Human Resources Development Canada offices

Many jobs are posted either on billboards or on self-serve computers at your local Human Resources Development Canada (HRDC) office. The Canadian government runs HRDC offices throughout Canada. They provide information and services for people looking for work. Some offer free use of computers, printers, the Internet, telephones, fax service, and resource libraries. They may offer workshops on how to prepare a résumé or look for work, as well as computer training and other courses.

HRDC also runs the Job Bank, and the Electronic Labour Exchange (ELE), an Internet site that matches jobs to people and people to jobs. Employers use the exchange to advertise a job and you can use it to advertise your skills to thousands of potential employers. The Internet address for the Electronic Labour Exchange is http://www.ele-spe.org

Another Internet site, which may be useful, is "Work search." This is an easy-to-use site, which can help you with all aspects of looking for work. The Internet address for this site is www.worksearch.gc.ca. The HRDC youth InfoLine is 1-800-935-5555.

You can find the nearest Human Resources Development Canada office listed in the blue pages of the telephone book, under Human Resources Development Canada.

Using the newspaper and other resources

Many jobs are listed in newspapers. Look in the classified advertisements section under "Help Wanted" and "Careers". There may also be a separate career section in the weekend paper.

Libraries are also helpful. They have books on how to find a job or write a résumé, and they often keep directories of businesses across Canada or in your area. These publications can help you to find information about potential employers. Their "periodical" section will also have copies of various weekly magazines, which provide new listings of jobs across Canada. You can also access the Internet at most public libraries. Ask for more information at the reference desk.

"Networking" is also a popular way of finding a job in Canada. This means contacting all the people you know, including your friends and relatives, and letting them know you are looking for work. This may help you to find a job, which is not actually advertised anywhere. Job-finding clubs run by immigrant-serving organizations may also be useful.

There are also private job placement agencies, which may be able to help you find permanent, temporary or contract work. Remember that since employers pay a fee to use these agencies, your salary may be somewhat lower than it would be if you found the job by yourself. These agencies are listed in the yellow pages of the telephone book. Look under "Employment Agencies."

Documents and foreign credentials

You may need Canadian qualifications to work at a licensed trade or profession. You may have to write an examination or work as a trainee to qualify. The requirements vary from province to province and from profession to profession. You might want to contact the national and/or provincial association, which looks after accreditation in your profession or trade. You can also contact the Canadian Information Centre for International Credentials, or other international credentials evaluations services. These are listed in the pamphlet *Key Information Sources* in the pocket at the back of this brochure.

Getting paid

Employers have the choice to pay their workers every week, every two weeks or once a month. You can be paid in cash, by cheque or by direct deposit to your bank account. Your pay stub (the piece of paper attached to your pay cheque) shows how much you earned. It also lists any money taken off (deductions) for federal and provincial taxes, pension plans, employment insurance, and any other items.

Working for yourself

More and more Canadians are working for themselves and running home-based businesses. You too might want to join this fast-growing group of entrepreneurs and go into business for yourself, or with a partner. Numerous information resources are available to you.

The Canadian Bankers Association offers a free publication entitled: *Starting a Small Business.* This contains most of the information you will need at the beginning. You can order this by calling their toll-free number: 1-800-263-0231.

The Business Development Bank of Canada also provides a book for newcomers interested in working for themselves, called *Starting a Business in Canada: A Guide for New Canadians.* They also offer management training, counseling and planning services for entrepreneurs. Call their toll-free number for more information: 1-888-463-6232 or visit their website at http://www.bdc.ca

Canada Business Service Centres provide a central resource for Canadian business information, especially government information. You can find them in every province, and territory. They offer service on the Internet, or you can speak directly to a business information officer. To find the Canada Business Service Centre nearest you, look in the blue pages of your telephone book under the federal government.

The *Small Business Loans Act* helps small businesses get loans from banks and other lenders. Contact Industry Canada in the federal government listings in the blue pages of your telephone book for more information.

Business and travel

Although the Canadian government realizes that travel is often part of doing business, you may lose your permanent resident status if you stay outside of the country for more than 183 days in a year. Before you leave for business, you should check with the CIC Call Centre.

If you are an entrepreneur who has been admitted to Canada on certain conditions, Citizenship and Immigration Canada will check to see how your business is doing. The Department will also provide special counseling services to help you. If after two years you have not fulfilled the conditions under which you were admitted, you and your dependants might be asked to leave. Remember, this only applies to those who come in as entrepreneurs under certain terms and conditions.

Daycare

When you do find work, you must remember that it is illegal in Canada to leave children under the age of 12 at home by themselves. You may need to pay someone to look after your children while you work. There are several options you can look into, such as licensed day care centres, home-based day care, nursery schools, and "drop-in" day care centres. You can also hire someone to come into your home and look after your children. Look in the yellow pages under "Day Nurseries" or "Day Care." Also check the classified advertisements section of the newspaper under "Employment Wanted" to find a caregiver in your area. Government-subsidized daycare exists for low-income families.

Labour laws and human rights

In Canada there are provincial and federal labour laws designed to protect employees and employers. These laws set minimum wage levels, health and safety standards, hours of work, maternity leave, annual paid vacations and provide protection for children. There are also human rights laws, which protect employees from unfair treatment by employers based on sex, age, race, religion or disability.

You also have the right to join a labour union in Canada. Unions negotiate wages, hours of work and working conditions. Union fees will be deducted from your salary.

If you feel you are being treated unfairly by your employer, you may seek advice and/or assistance from an officer of the Ministry of Labour in the province where you work. You can also contact the Canadian Human Rights Commission or a Human Resources Development Canada office, where you can talk to a federal government labour affairs officer.

Volunteering

You might wish to help out in an agency or community organization as a volunteer. This means that you volunteer your time but you do not get paid. However, volunteering can help you develop Canadian job experience, get a practical knowledge of the Canadian workplace, practice your English or French and make new friends, as well as help others. You can find volunteer centres in the yellow pages of your telephone book, or contact your local community agency.

An example of volunteering is the Host Program. The Canadian government funds the Host Program to help newcomers adapt, settle and integrate into Canadian life. Host volunteers are Canadians who offer their time to be with newcomers and introduce them to the Canadian way of life.

For more information on the Host Program, contact one of the local immigrant-serving organizations listed in the pamphlet called *Finding Help in Your Community*, in the back pocket of this guide.

☑ **Do you know that it is illegal to leave children under 12 at home alone?**

☑ **Have you applied for a Social Insurance Number card at the Human Resources Development Canada office?**

LEARNING ENGLISH OR FRENCH

- **Language Instruction for Newcomers to Canada (LINC)**
- **To find out more...**

*T*here are two official languages in Canada -- English and French. Almost everyone in Canada speaks at least one of these languages and millions of Canadians speak both. There are anglophone and francophone communities in every province and territory. English is the language of the majority everywhere in Canada, except in the province of Quebec where French is the official language. French is spoken in many communities in other provinces, especially New Brunswick, Ontario and Manitoba. New Brunswick is an officially bilingual province.

One of the most important skills you will need to adapt to life here in Canada is to speak English or French. Once you learn one or both of these languages, you will find it easier to get a job, to understand Canada, and to communicate with your children, who will be busy learning English or French at school. You will also need to know English or French to become a Canadian citizen.

There are many language courses available, and many of them are free. Sometimes these courses are called "ESL" for English as a Second Language courses, or "FSL," for French as a Second Language courses.

Language Instruction for Newcomers to Canada (LINC)

The Government of Canada, in cooperation with provincial governments, school boards, community colleges, and immigrant-serving organizations, offers free language training across the country to adult permanent residents. In most provinces, the name of the program is LINC. (In French this program is known as CLIC, for Cours de langue pour les immigrants au Canada.) LINC can also assess your current language skills, to find out which training program would be best for you.

LINC offers both full- and part-time classes, to suit your needs. Most LINC centres can also refer you to other non-LINC classes in your area, and some offer free childcare while you attend classes.

Remember, language classes are available for all the adults in your family, not just the person who may be looking for work.

To find out more...

To find out where you can get LINC classes in your area, you will find a listing of LINC assessment centres in the pamphlet called *Language Training*, in the back pocket of this guide. You could also contact your local immigrant-serving organization. They will likely refer you to a LINC assessment centre, which will then refer you to organizations offering LINC classes. You might also want to telephone your local school board directly to find out about classes in your community.

Most universities and community colleges also offer language classes, as well as some private language schools and community organizations. You can contact these groups directly for more information. Remember to ask about fees, since these courses may not be free.

☑ **Do you know where the LINC assessment centre is in your community?**

EDUCATION

- **Finding schools**
- **Enrolling your children**
- **Adult education**
- **To find out more...**

*C*hildren between 6 and 16 must attend school, and most of them go to public schools. Classes usually start in early September and end in late June. There is a two-week vacation at Christmas and one-week vacation in either February or March. Children attend school Monday to Friday, for about six hours per day. They usually bring their lunch with them.

There are also private schools, but these can be quite expensive. Public and separate (Catholic) schools are paid for through your taxes.

Finding schools

The best way to find out which schools your children should attend is by phoning the school boards in your area. These are listed under "Schools" in the yellow pages of your telephone book. This choice is usually based on where you live and which system you prefer.

Many schools are not within walking distance, and children often take school buses (provided by the school at minimal or no cost to you) or public transportation to get there. This is something to consider when choosing either a school or a place to live.

Enrolling your children

When you enroll your children, take their birth certificates or other identity documents to the school. If the originals of the documents are in languages other than English or French, you should have them translated into English or French. Also bring their Record of Landing (IMM 1000), passport and any former school and health records. You could also be asked for immunization records.

Adult education

Learning is a lifelong activity in Canada, and many Canadians continue to study as adults. Adult education is not free. Student loans are available through the universities and colleges. You may wish to train for a new job, or to improve the skills you already have. You may also wish to apprentice for a trade. The qualifications for many trades are different from province to province, and you must obtain a license before you can practice. Remember that some Canadian schools will not give credit for a course or diploma obtained outside Canada.

If you want information on continuing education, contact the school board, college or university in your community. Look these up in the yellow pages of the telephone book under "Schools," "Colleges," and "Universities." You can also get a list of the educational institutions in your area from an immigrant-serving organization.

You might also want to look up professional or trade associations in the province where you live for information on qualifications.

To find out more...

Other sources of information are:

- provincial departments of education;
- school boards;
- universities and community colleges;
- professional or trade associations;
- immigrant-serving organizations.

☑ **Are your children registered in school?**

☑ **Have your educational credentials been translated into English or French?**

TAXATION

- **Income tax**
- **Other taxes**
- **To find out more...**

*C*anadian residents can benefit from programs that have been paid for from their taxes and payroll contributions. These programs include social assistance for people in need; employment insurance for workers who have lost their jobs; worker's compensation for workers injured on the job; old-age pensions for citizens 65 years of age and older.

Income tax

Canadians pay a variety of taxes. Income tax is used by governments to provide services, such as roads, schools and health care. All residents of Canada are subject to income tax. Each year you must submit an Income Tax and Benefit Return to tell the government how much money you earned and how much tax you paid. Taxes are deducted automatically from most income you receive. If you paid too much, you will get a refund. If you paid too little, you will have to pay more.

Filing an income tax return is extremely important. You will need to file one each year to qualify for various government benefits, such as the Canada Child Tax Benefit. You can get the forms for the federal income tax from any post office or Canada Customs and Revenue Agency tax services office. Canada Customs and Revenue Agency has several publications for newcomers, which should be helpful. (Call 1-800 959-2221 or visit http://www.ccra-adrc.gc.ca) They also have volunteers who can help you fill out your tax forms, under the Community Volunteer Income Tax Program. This is a free service. The deadline for completing your tax return is April 30 of each year. Remember, if you lived in Quebec during the year you will also have to file a separate provincial tax return.

Other taxes

Whenever you buy something, a Goods and Services Tax (GST) will be added to the price. This includes everything from socks to a new house. You may also pay a provincial sales tax (PST), which varies from province to province. If you own your own home, you will also pay property and school taxes. For more information on these taxes, contact either your local school board or your municipal government.

To find out more...

Contact

- Canada Customs and Revenue Agency,
- the provincial Ministry of Revenue, or
- your local school boards, all of which are listed in the telephone book.

CANADIAN LAW

- **Police**
- **Legal services**
- **Children's rights**
- **Women's rights**
- **Domestic violence**
- **Seniors' rights**

*C*anada is governed by an organized system of laws. These laws are created by governments, which are chosen freely by the people. The law in Canada applies to everyone, including the police, judges, politicians, and members of the government. The main purposes of our laws are to provide order in society, to provide a peaceful way to settle disputes, and to express the values and beliefs of Canadian society. Everyone in Canada whether a citizen, or a permanent resident has equal access to the justice system.

Police

The police are there to keep people safe and enforce the law. You can ask the police for help in all kinds of situations -- if there's been an accident, if someone has stolen something from you, if you are a victim of assault, if you see a crime taking place, if someone you know has gone missing, etc.

There are different types of police in Canada, including provincial police departments and the Royal Canadian Mounted Police, who enforce federal laws. Remember, the police are there to help you. Don't hesitate to call 911 or 0 for the operator to contact your local police force in an emergency.

If for some reason you are questioned by the police or arrested, do not resist. Remember, in Canada, you are presumed innocent until proven guilty. Communicate as clearly as possible and look directly at the officer. Be ready to show some kind of identification. If you are taken into custody you have the right to know why and to have a lawyer and a translator, if needed. Under Canadian law, it is a serious crime to try to bribe the police by offering money, gifts or services in exchange for special treatment.

Legal services

If you need a lawyer to protect your interests in court, then you can hire one, for a fee. You may also be entitled to free legal services, or "legal aid," depending on your income. You will find the numbers for provincial legal aid in the booklet called *Key Information Sources* in the back pocket of this guide. An immigrant-serving organization will also be able to tell you where and how to obtain these services.

Children's rights

Parents in Canada have a legal duty to provide their children with the necessities of life until they reach age 16. It is illegal in Canada to abuse your children either physically, psychologically, or sexually. All forms of child abuse are serious crimes. Abuse can include spanking children enough to cause bruises, terrorizing or humiliating them, any kind of sexual contact, and neglect. Police, doctors, teachers and children's aid workers will take action if they think children are being harmed. In serious cases, children can be taken away from their parents. Some cultural practices are not acceptable in Canada. For instance, all forms of female genital mutilation (FGM) are prohibited under Canadian law.

Women's rights

In Canada, men and women are equal. They have the same rights, as outlined in the *Canadian Charter of Rights and Freedoms.* Discrimination against women and violence towards women are both against the law. Women who are abused by their husbands can seek help for themselves and their children in community shelters. They are also entitled to legal protection to keep them safe.

There are a number of organizations in Canada, which work to safeguard and promote the rights of women, and some of these organizations work to help immigrant women in particular. Your local immigrant-serving agency will be able to provide you with the names of these organizations. Information on legal rights and shelters can be found near the front of your telephone book under "Distress Centres," "Child Abuse," or "Sexual Assault."

Domestic violence

Violence towards any person -- man, woman or child -- is against the law in Canada. No one has the right to hit or threaten people or to force them into sexual activities. The law applies no matter who it is -- wife/husband, partner, girlfriend/boyfriend, parent, or another relative.

If you or your children are being abused, call the police at 911 or your local emergency number. They can help you find medical help or drive you to a safe place, if you wish. Emergency shelters, counseling and free legal advice are available for adults and children who are being abused. There are also Rape Crisis and Sexual Assault Support Centres listed in the first few pages of the telephone book. They are there to help you. In many Canadian cities there are also 24-hour-a-day telephone help lines, if you just need someone to talk to. They can also refer you to the help you need.

Many community centres also offer counseling for abusive partners who are seeking help, for families who wish to stay together, and for children.

Seniors' rights

A senior citizen is someone 65 years of age or older. If you are a senior, you may be entitled to certain government benefits, such as the Old Age Security pension (OAS) and the Guaranteed Income Supplement (GIS). In order to qualify, you must meet certain residence requirements. You may also be eligible for old age security benefits from your former country. Some provinces supplement these plans, and offer extra benefits such as prescription drug plans. For information, call 1-800 277-9914 (toll-free). If you have a hearing or speech impairment and you use a TDD/TTY device, please call 1-800 255-4786. The French toll-free number is 1-800 277-9915.

Many businesses also offer special rates for senior citizens, or special areas where seniors can be served more comfortably.

☑ Do you know that violence towards any person -- man, woman or child -- is against the law in Canada?

☑ Do you know that the practice of female genital mutilation (FGM) is against the law?

TRANSPORTATION

- **Getting a driver's licence**
- **Buying a car**
- **Use of seat belts**
- **Car seats for children**
- **In case of an accident**
- **To find out more...**

Getting a driver's licence

You ou need a valid driver's licence to drive a car in Canada, and these are issued by the province or territory where you live. Your foreign driver's licence may be valid for a short time after you arrive in Canada, but eventually you will need to take a Canadian driving test to remain licensed. This will help you to learn about the rules of the road in Canada. You may also want to obtain an International Driving Permit. Find out more from your provincial ministry of transportation or from your provincial motor vehicle licensing agency.

Driving lessons are available from private companies, for a fee. You may want to have a few lessons before you take your test. Look in the yellow pages under "Driving Instruction."

Remember: It is a legal requirement to carry your driver's licence with you whenever you drive. You should also carry your car registration and vehicle permit with you. It is good advice to carry a copy of your car insurance certificate.

Buying a car

Cars can cost a lot of money, whether they are used or new. Make sure you can afford the upkeep, the gas, the monthly payments and the costs of registering and insuring it. Some Canadians opt to lease cars. Leasing can be handy, but there are a number of hidden costs involved, such as administrative fees or handling taxes. Whichever option you choose make sure you understand exactly what your financial obligations are.

Car insurance is another major expense. All cars must be registered with the provincial motor vehicle licensing agency where you live, and must be insured. This is the law. Car insurance can be expensive, but it protects you and other drivers in case of an accident. You buy insurance through private insurance companies, listed in the yellow pages under "Insurance". Some provinces also sell insurance through provincial corporations. Shop around for the best rates. An accident-free record will help you get a better insurance rate. In most provinces, you can obtain more information by calling the Insurance Bureau of Canada or visiting their website at http://www.ibc.ca

Use of seat belts

You and your passengers must wear seat belts at all times when you are driving in Canada. This is the law. The use of a seat belt can save your life in an accident, and you can be fined for not wearing one.

Car seats for children

Babies and children who are too small to wear seat belts safely must be placed in car seats whenever you drive. These can also help to save lives in case of an accident. There are different types of car seats for different ages and weights. For example, infants must be placed in special seats that face the back of the car. Children over 18 kg need a booster seat.

In case of an accident

Call 911 or your local emergency number right away if you need medical help. Stay where you are, and get someone to call the police. You should also report the accident immediately to your car insurance company. It is also important to exchange your name, address, and telephone number, as well as your insurance and driver's licence numbers with the other driver. Never leave the scene of an accident, especially if you have hit someone. This is a serious offence known as "hit-and-run."

☑ **Do you have a valid driver's licence?**

☑ **Do you have car insurance?**

☑ **Do you have a car seat for your child?**

To find out more...

Contact the public transit organizations, provincial ministries of transportation, provincial motor vehicle licensing offices or insurance associations listed in the telephone book.

KEEPING IN TOUCH

- **Canada Post**
- **Returning Resident Permits**

Canada Post

*C*anada's mail is handled by the Canada Post Corporation. To send mail, use a postage stamp. You can buy postage stamps at any post office. They are also sold in many drug stores, hotel lobbies, airports, railway stations, bus terminals and some newsstands. The cost of the stamp is based on the weight and size of the letter or package, and where your mail is going. When you send something to an address in Canada, remember to include the six-digit postal code for that address, and also a return address. This will speed up delivery. If you are sending something overseas, you must use the special code for that country. You can find these at a post office.

Mail your letter or small package either at a post office or in the red Canada Post mailboxes you will find on streets and in shopping malls all across Canada. Take large parcels to a post office.

Canada Post offers many other services too, such as express delivery, postal money orders and insurance for very important mail. This insurance can protect your mail against loss or damage. Express delivery is more expensive than regular letter mail. Check the rates at the nearest Canada Post office. There are also private special delivery or courier services. Look these up under "Courier" in the yellow pages of the telephone book. Mail is distributed daily from Monday to Friday, except on official holidays. This includes home delivery, to post office boxes, or to community mailboxes. If you want to send a telegram, look up "Telegram Services" in the yellow pages for more information.

Returning Resident Permits

From time to time you may wish to leave Canada to visit your relatives. If you are not a Canadian citizen, and you plan to be outside Canada for more than 183 days in a year, you will need to apply for a

Returning Resident Permit. If you don't have one, you could be refused entry into Canada when you return. You could lose your permanent resident status. Before you go you should telephone the CIC Call Centre for information and an application form. Remember there is a processing fee for this service.

BECOMING A CANADIAN

- **The rights and responsibilities of citizenship**
- **How to apply**

*A*lthough you can't apply for Canadian citizenship until you have lived in Canada for at least three years, you can be thinking about what it means from the moment you arrive. Canadians believe that Canada is a special place. Most Canadians agree with the United Nations that "Canada is the best country in the world in which to live."

To obtain Canadian citizenship, you will have to demonstrate a deep commitment to this country.

- You will need to meet the physical residence requirements. You must live in Canada for at least three years before applying to become a citizen.

- You will need to have sufficient knowledge of either English or French.

- You will need to demonstrate your knowledge of Canada and the responsibilities and privileges of citizenship.

- You must be 18 years of age or older to apply as an individual.

The rights and responsibilities of citizenship

For many newcomers, this gift of citizenship, this special sense of belonging, is a goal that guides much of what they do every day. It involves pride. A belief in equality and diversity. Respect for others. It means accepting the shared values that make Canadians who they are, and respecting both the rights and the privileges of being Canadian.

Canadian citizenship is precious and respected. Citizenship is a contract between you and your country, to share in the rights and privileges citizenship offers, and to fully carry out the responsibilities that go with it.

How to apply

To obtain information and an application kit to become a Canadian citizen visit http://www.cic.gc.ca or contact the CIC Call Centre. For the telephone number, refer to the section **Basic Services:** Citizenship and Immigration Canada (CIC) Call Centre

A Few last words

We hope this guide has given you some understanding of what it means to live in Canada. We've tried to combine practical information with an idea of the values and beliefs, which keep us together as Canadians, and as a country. As you journey towards Canadian citizenship, we sincerely hope this information helps you feel at home, feel that special sense of belonging. We are a nation of newcomers, and we welcome you to our family.

> *"I've become a Canadian citizen and feel proud, happy and lucky. I was so grateful to Canada. I had missed my childhood and now was starting another period of my life. I think every Canadian should be proud. Even if I am a different colour, I have my rights. I am a Canadian."*

Channa Som, Survivor, Cambodian "killing fields."

> *"To me, Canada is a unique combination of many things and many people from many places. It's a creation that the world -- and we -- should cherish and nourish.*

Serge Radchuk, originally from Ukraine.

> *"I'll never forget the immigration officer I met at Dorval. He had an enormous, long ginger handlebar moustache that looked like a flaming sword. This man turned to me and spontaneously said, 'Welcome to Canada.' I was so touched that he knew I needed some reassurance and that he would understand my feeling of nervousness."*

Hubert de Santana, originally from Kenya.

Please Note

This guide contains information that was current at the time of publication. It features information from many sources, and should not be confused with official statements of policy or programming. The Government of Canada is not responsible for information that changes between printings.

Living in Canada: Your checklist

With so much to remember, we decided to create a checklist to help you to get the important things done first. We hope you find it useful.

In Your First Few Weeks

You will need to...

- Exchange your money for Canadian currency
- Find temporary accommodation
- Have some identification (ID) with you
- Apply for private Health Insurance
- Get a map of the area and find out about transportation in your area
- Get your own telephone book
- Contact an immigrant-serving organization in your community
- Fill out the forms for a Social Insurance Number card and a Health Insurance card

In Your First Few Months

You will need to...

- Find permanent housing
- Get a telephone installed
- Register your children in school
- Get a family doctor
- Have your children immunized
- Open a bank account
- Look for a job
- Carry your address and telephone number with you
- Try to make friends -- join the Host Program
- Know where the Language Instruction for Newcomers (LINC) assessment centre is in your community and register for language classes
- Apply for the Canada Child Tax Benefit; call 1-800 387-1193

In Your First Year

You will need to...

- Get a valid driver's licence
- Practice and improve your language skills
- Register for adult continuing education classes
- Take time to relax and participate in community activities
- Understand your rights and responsibilities under Canadian law
- Know that you can apply for Canadian citizenship after living in Canada for three years

Finding Help in Your Community

$\mathcal{T}$ here are many organizations, which provide services designed for newcomers to Canada. In fact, your local immigrant serving organization should be your first point of contact. Many of these organizations across the country are listed in this directory, organized by province.

Since Quebec looks after many aspects of its immigration program, this pamphlet does not attempt to cover services in that province. However, it does list the phone numbers for the *ministère des Relations avec les citoyens et de l'Immigration,* which offers many services to newcomers in Quebec. If you are living in, or planning to move to Quebec, you may wish to pick up their guide for newcomers, entitled: *Vivre au QUÉBEC!*

You may also wish to refer to the other two pamphlets in the back pocket of your guide: Key Information Sources, and Language Training.

Remember when you use the telephone, speak slowly and clearly, and have a pen or pencil and some paper to write down information. You may be referred to another phone number, or be given other useful information.

KEY IMMIGRANT SERVING
ORGANIZATIONS ACROSS CANADA

Newfoundland

Association for New Canadians
P.0. Box 2031, Station C
St. John's, Nfld. A1C 5R6

Tel: 709-722-9680

Nova Scotia

YMCA Newcomer's Centre
3663 Dutch Village Road
Halifax, N.S. B3K 3B7

Tel: 902-457-9622

Metropolitan Immigrant Settlement Association
2131 Gottingen Street, Suite 200
Halifax, N.S. B3K 5Z7

Tel: 902-423-3607

Prince Edward Island

PEI Association for Newcomers to Canada
179 Queen Street
Mailing address: P.O. Box 2846,
Charlottetown, PEI C1A 8C4

Tel: 902-628-6009

New Brunswick

Multicultural Association of Fredericton
123 York Street, Suite 201
Fredericton, N.B. E3B 3N6
Tel: 506-457-4038

Multicultural Association of Greater Moncton Area
1299A Mountain Road, Suite 2
Moncton, N.B. E1C 2T9
506-858-9659

Saint John YM/YWCA
19-25 Hazen Avenue
Saint John, N.B. E2L 3G6
506-646-2389

Quebec

To contact immigrant serving organizations in the province of Quebec, contact the *ministère des Relations avec les citoyens et de l'Immigration* (MRCI). MRCI is organized by region:

Carrefours d'intégration - Island of Montréal

North Island
255, boulevard Crémazie Est
8e et 9e étages
Montréal (Québec) H2M 1L5
(514) 864-9191

West Island
181, boulevard Hymus
2e et 3e étages
Point-Claire (Québec) H9R 5P4
(514) 864-9191

East Island
8000, boulevard Langelier
6e et 7e étages
Saint-Léonard (Québec) H1P 3K2
(514) 864-9191

South Island
800, boulevard de Maisonneuve Est
(Place Dupuis), rez-de-chaussée)
Montréal (Québec) H2L 4L8
(514) 864-9191

Direction régionale de l'Outaouais,
de l'Abitibi-Témiscamingue et du Nord-du-Québec

4 rue Taschereau, suite 430
Hull, Québec J8Y 2V5
819-772-3021 or
1-888-295-9095

Direction régionale de Laval, des Laurentides, et de Lanaudière
800, boulevard Chomedey
Tour C, bureau 200
Laval, Québec H7V 3Y4
450-681-2593 or
1-800-375-7426

Direction régionale de la Capitale-Nationale et l'Est du Québec
930, chemin Ste-Foy
Québec, Québec G1S 2L4
418-643-1435 or
1-888-643-1435

Direction régionale de l'Estrie, de la Mauricie et du Centre-du-Québec
740, rue Galt Ouest, bureau 400
Sherbrooke, Québec J1H 1Z3
819-820-3606 or 1-888-879-4288

Direction régionale de la Montérégie
3e étage
2, blvd Désaulniers
St-Lambert, Québec J4P 1L2
450-466-4461 or 1-888-287-5819

Bureau de Trois-Rivières
100, rue Laviolette, R.C. 26
Trois-Rivières, Québec G9A 5S9
819-371-6011 or 1-888-879-4294

Bureau de Jonquière
3950 boulevard Harvey
Jonquière, Québec G7X 8L6
418-695-8144

Ontario

Social Development Council Ajax, Pickering
134 Commercial Avenue
Ajax, Ontario L1S 2H5
905-686-2661

Barrie YMCA Immigrant Services
22 Grove Street West
Barrie, Ontario L4N 1M7
705-726-6421 ext. 264

Quinte United Immigrant Services
32 Bridge Street East
Belleville, Ontario K8N 5N9
613-968-7723

Newcomer Information Centre, Centre for Language
Training and Assessment Brampton Civic Centre
150 Central Park Drive, Suite 200
Brampton, Ontario L6T 1B4
905-270-6000

Brampton Neighbourhood Resource Centre
168 Kennedy Road South
Units 3 and 4
Brampton, Ontario L6W 3G6
905-452-1262

Catholic Cross-Cultural Services
37 George Street North, Suite 403
Brampton, Ontario L6X 1R5
905-457-7740

Immigrant Settlement and
Counseling Services of Brantford
320 North Park Street, Unit 2
Brantford, Ontario N3R 4L4
519-753-9830

YMCA of Cambridge
250 Hespeler Road
Cambridge, Ontario N1R 3H3
519-621-3250

Arab Community Centre
5468 Dundas Street West, Suite 324
Etobicoke, Ontario M9B 6E3
416-231-7746

Dejinta Beesha
8 Taber Road
Etobicoke, Ontario M9W 3A4
416-743-1286

Rexdale Women's Centre
8 Taber Road, 2nd Floor
Etobicoke, Ontario M9W 3A4
416-745-0062

Polycultural Immigrant and Community Services
3363 Bloor Street West
Etobicoke, Ontario M8X 1G2
416-233-0055

Guelph and District Multicultural Centre
214 Speedvale Avenue West, Unit 7
Guelph, Ontario N1H 1C4
519-836-2222

Settlement and Integration Services Organization of Hamilton
360 James Street North
Hamilton, Ontario L8L 1H5
905-521-9917

Kingston and District Immigrant Services
322 Brock Street
Kingston, Ontario K7L 1S9
613-548-3302

Mennonite Central Committee of Ontario
50 Kent Avenue
Kitchener, Ontario N2G 3R1
519-745-8458

Kitchener-Waterloo YMCA
301-276 King Street West
Kitchener, Ontario N2G 1B6
519-579-9622

London Cross-Cultural Learner Centre
717 Dundas Street East
London, Ontario N5W 2Z5
519-432-1133

Catholic Cross-Cultural Services
90 Dundas Street West, site 204
Mississauga , Ontario L5B 2T5
905-273-4140

Dixie-Bloor Neighbourhood Resource Centre
3439 Fieldgate Drive
Mississauga, Ontario L4X 2J4
905-629-1873

India Rainbow Community Services of Peel
3038 Hurontario Street, Suite 206
Mississauga, Ontario L5B 3B9
905-275-2369

Malton Neighbourhood Services
7200 Goreway Drive
Mississauga, Ontario L4T 2T7
905-677-6270
905-672-3660

Inter-Cultural Neighbourhood Social Services
3050 Confederation Parkway
Mississauga, Ontario L5B 3Z6
905-273-4884

Jewish Immigrant Aid Services of Canada
4600 Bathurst Street, Suite 325
North York, Ontario M2R 3V3
416-630-6481

Northwood Neighbourhood Services (C.S.)
2528A Jane Street
Wycliffe Jane Plaza
North York, Ontario
416-748-0788

Halton Multicultural Association
635 4th Line, Unit 48

Oakville, Ontario L6L 5W4
905-842-2486

Catholic Immigration Centre
219 Argyle Avenue
Ottawa, Ontario K2P 2H4
613-232-9634

Jewish Family Services of Ottawa-Carleton
1774 Kerr Avenue, Suite 230
Ottawa, Ontario K2A 1R9
613-722-2225

Lebanese and Arab Social Services Agency of Ottawa-Carleton
151 Slater Street, Suite 707
Ottawa, Ontario K1P 5H3
613-236-0003

Ottawa Carleton Immigrant Services Organization
959 Wellington Street
Ottawa, Ontario KIY 4W1
613-725-0202

Ottawa Chinese Community Service Centre
391 Bank Street, 2nd Floor
Ottawa, Ontario K2P 1Y3
613-235-4875

New Canadians Centre - Peterborough
205 Sherbrooke Street, Unit D
Peterborough, Ontario K9J 2N2
705-743-0882

Catholic Community Services of York Region
21 Dunlop Street
Richmond Hill, Ontario L4C 2M6
905-770-7040

Folk Arts Council of St. Catharines
85 Church Street
St. Catharines, Ontario L2R 3C7
905-685-6589

Tropicana Community Services Organization
670 Progress Avenue, Unit 14
Scarborough, Ontario M1H 3A4
416-439-9009

South Asian Family Support Services (SAFS)
1200 Markham Road, Suite 214
Scarborough, Ontario M1H 3C3
416-431-4847

Catholic Cross-Cultural Services
780 Birchmount Road, Unit 3
Scarborough, Ontario M1K 5H4
416-757-7010

Centre for Information and Community Services of Ontario (CICS)
3852 Finch Avenue East, Suite 310
Scarborough, Ontario M1T 3T9
416-292-7510

Sudbury Multicultural Folk Arts Association
196 Van Horne Street
Sudbury, Ontario P3E 1E5
705-674-0795

Thunder Bay Multicultural Association
17 North Court Street
Thunder Bay, Ontario P7A 4T4
807-345-0551

Afghan Women's Counseling and Integration
Community Support Organization
2333 Dundas Street West, Suite 205A
Toronto, Ontario M6R 3A6
416-588-3585

Bloor Information and Life Skills Centre
672 Dupont Street, Suite 314
Toronto, Ontario M6G 1Z6
416-531-4613

Canadian Centre for Victims of Torture
192-194 Jarvis Street, 2nd Floor
Toronto, Ontario M5B 2B7
416-363-1066

Canadian Ukrainian Immigrant Aid Services
2150 Bloor Street West, Suite 96
Toronto, Ontario M6S 1M8
416-767-0036

Catholic Cross-Cultural Services
10 St. Mary Street, Suite 410
Toronto, Ontario M4Y 1P9
416-324-8225

Harriet Tubman Community Organization Inc.
2975 Don Mills Road
Toronto, Ontario M2J 3B7
416-496-2044

Centre for Spanish-Speaking Peoples
1004 Bathurst Street
Toronto, Ontario M5R 3G7
416-533-8545

COFTM Centre Francophone
20 Lower Spadina Avenue
Toronto, Ontario M5V 2Z1
416-203-1220

COSTI-IIAS Immigrant Services
1710 Dufferin Street
Toronto, Ontario M6E 3P2
416-658-1600

CultureLink
160 Springhurst Avenue, Suite 300
Toronto, Ontario M6K 1C2
416-588-6288

Ethiopian Association in Toronto, Inc.
2057 Danforth Avenue, 3rd Floor
Toronto, Ontario M4C 1J8
416-694-1522

Jamaican Canadian Association
995 Arrow Road
Toronto, Ontario M9M 2Z5
416-746-5772

Kababayan Community Service Centre
1313 Queen Street West, Suite 133
Toronto, Ontario M6K 1L8
416-532-3888

Mennonite New Life Centre
1774 Queen Street East
Toronto, Ontario M4L 1G7
416-699-4527

Newcomer Information Centre,
YMCA of Greater Toronto
42 Charles Street East, 3rd Floor
Toronto, Ontario M4Y 1T4
416-928-3362

MIDAYNTA
1992 Yonge Street, Suite 203
Toronto, Ontario M4S 1Z8
416-544-1992
416-440-0520

Tropicana Community Services Organization
670 Progress Avenue, Unit 14
Scarborough, Ontario M1H 3A4
(416) 439-9009

Riverdale Immigrant Women's Centre
1326 Gerrard Street East, Suite 100
Toronto, Ontario M4L 1Z1
416-465-6021

Scadding Court Community Centre
707 Dundas Street West
Toronto, Ontario M5T 2W6
416-392-0335

South Asian Women's Centre
1332 Bloor Street West
Toronto, Ontario M6H 1P2
416-537-2276

Tamil Eelam Society of Canada
861 Broadview Avenue
Toronto, Ontario M4K 2P9
416-463-7647

Thorncliffe Park Neighbourhood Services
18 Thorncliffe Park Drive
Toronto, Ontario M4H 1N7
416-421-3054

Toronto Chinese Community Services Association
310 Spadina Avenue, Suite 301
Toronto, Ontario M5T 2E8
416-977-4026

Toronto Organization for Domestic Workers' Rights (INTERCEDE)
234 Eglinton Avenue East, Suite 205
Toronto, Ontario M4P 1K5
416 483 1551

Vietnamese Association of Toronto
1364 Dundas Street West
Toronto, Ontario M6J 1Y2
416-536-3611

Woodgreen Community Centre of Toronto
835 Queen Street East
Toronto, Ontario M4M 1H9
416-469-5211

Working Women Community Centre
533A Gladstone Avenue
Toronto, Ontario M6H 3J1
416-532-2824

Lakeshore Area Multi-Service
Project Inc.
185 Fifth Street
Toronto, Ontario M8V 2Z5
416-252-6471

YMCA of Metro Toronto
(Korean Community Services)
721 Bloor Street West, Suite 303
Toronto, Ontario M6G 1L5
416-538-9412

Youth Assisting Youth
1992 Yonge Street, Suite 300
Toronto, Ontario M4S 1Z7
416-932-1919

Afghan Association of Ontario
29 Pemican Court, #6
Weston, Ontario M9M 2Z3
416-744-9289

New Canadians' Centre
Windsor Essex County Family YMCA
511 Pelisser Street
Windsor, Ontario N9A 4L2
519-256-7330

Multicultural Council of Windsor
and Essex County
245 Janette Avenue
Windsor, Ontario N9A 4Z2
519-255-1127

The Job Search Workshops in Ontario
1-800-813-2614

Manitoba

International Centre of Winnipeg
406 Edmonton Street, 2nd floor
Winnipeg, Manitoba R3B 2M2
204-943-9158

Jewish Child and Family Services
Suite C200-123 Doncaster Street
Winnipeg, Manitoba R3N 2B2
204-477-7430

Lao Association of Manitoba
7-983 Arlington Street
Winnipeg, Manitoba R3E 2E6
204-774-1115

Indochina Chinese Association of Manitoba
648 McGee Street
Winnipeg, Manitoba R3E 1W8
204-772-3107

Immigrant Women Association of Manitoba
200-323 Portage Avenue
Winnipeg, Manitoba R3B 2C1
204-989-5800

Philippine Association of Manitoba
88 Juno Street
Winnipeg, Manitoba
204-772-7210

Employment Projects for Women
990-167 Lombard Avenue
Winnipcg, Manitoba R3B 0V3
204-949-5300

Success Skills Centre
616-1661 Portage Avenue
Winnipeg, Manitoba R3J 3T7
204-786-3200

Ukrainian Canadian Congress
456 Main Street
Winnipeg, Manitoba R3B 1B6
204-942-4627

Black Youth Helpline
P.O. Box 11
1631 St-Mary's Road
Winnipeg, Manitoba R2M 4A5
204-339-2769

Citizenship Council of Manitoba
406 Edmonton Street, 2nd Floor
Winnipeg, Manitoba R3B 2M2
204-943-9158

Manitoba Interfaith
406 Edmonton Street, 2nd floor
Winnipeg, Manitoba R3B 2M2
204-943-9158

Saskatchewan

Moose Jaw Multicultural Council
60 Athabasca Street East
Moose Jaw, Saskatchewan S6H 0L2
306-693-4677

Prince Albert Multicultural Council
17 11th Street West
Prince Albert, Saskatchewan S6V 3A8
306-922-0405

Regina Open Door Society
1855 Smith Street
Regina, Saskatchewan S4P 2N5
306-352-3500

Saskatoon Open Door Society
311 4th Avenue North
Saskatoon, Saskatchewan S7K 2L8
306-653-4464

Alberta

Calgary Catholic Immigration Society
3rd Floor, 120-17 Avenue SW
Calgary, Alberta T2S 2T2
403-262-2006

Calgary Immigrant Aid Society
12th Floor, 910-7 Avenue SW
Calgary, Alberta T2P 3N8
403-265-1120

Calgary Immigrant Women's Association
300, 750 - 11 Street SW
Calgary, Alberta T2P 3N7
403-263-4414

Calgary Immigrant Development and
Educational Advancement Society
203-4310 17th Avenue SE
Calgary, Alberta T2A 0T4
403-235-3666

Calgary Mennonite Centre for Newcomers
201, 3517 - 17 Avenue SE
Calgary, Alberta T2A 0R5
403-569-0409

The Calgary Bridge Foundation for Youth
4112-4 Street NW
Calgary, Alberta T2K 1A2
403-230-7745

Catholic Social Services
10709-105 Street
Edmonton, Alberta T5H 2X3
780-424-3545

Changing Together - A Centre for Immigrant Women
#103, 10010 - 107A Avenue
Edmonton, Alberta T5H 4H8
780-421-0175

Indo-Canadian Women's Association
335 Tower II, Millbourne Mall
Edmonton, Alberta T6K 3L2
780-490-0477

Edmonton Catholic Schools
10915-110 Street
Edmonton, Alberta T5H 3E3
780-426-4375

Edmonton Chinese Community Services Centre
9540 - 102 Avenue
Edmonton, Alberta T5H 0E3
780-429-3111

Edmonton Immigrant Services Association
11240 - 79 Street
Edmonton, Alberta T5B 2K1
780-474-8445

Edmonton Mennonite Centre for Newcomers
#101, 10010 - 107A Avenue
Edmonton, Alberta T5H 4H8
780-424-7709

Edmonton Public School Board
6703-112 Street
Edmonton, Alberta T6H 3J9
780-431-5479

Millwoods Welcome Centre for Immigrants
335 Tower II, Millbourne Mall
Edmonton, Alberta T6K 3L2
780-462-6924

New Home Immigration and Settlement
572 Hermitage Road
Edmonton, Alberta T5A 4N2
780-456-4663

YMCA of Wood Buffalo
#200, 9913 Biggs Avenue
Fort McMurray, Alberta T9H 1S2
780-743-2970

The Reading Network - Grande Prairie Regional College
Lower Level, 9920 - 100 Avenue
Grande Prairie, Alberta T8V 0T9
780-538-4363

Lethbridge Family Services - Immigrant Services
508-6th Street South
Lethbridge, Alberta T1J 2E2
403-320-1589
403-317-7654 (FAX)

SAAMIS Immigration Services
177 12 Street NE
Medicine Hat, Alberta T1A 5T6

403-504-1188
Fax 403-504-1211

Catholic Social Services - Red Deer
5104-48th Avenue
Red Deer, Alberta T4N 3T8
403-347-8844

Catholic Social Services
202-5000 Gaetz Avenue
Red Deer, Alberta T4N 6C2
403-346-8818

Central Alberta Refugee Effort (C.A.R.E.) Committee
202-5000 Gaetz Avenue
Red Deer, Alberta T4N 6C2
403-346-8818

British Columbia

Abbotsford Community Services
2420 Montrose Avenue
Abbotsford, BC V2S 3S9
604-859-7081

Mennonite Central Committee of BC
31414 Marshall Road, Box 2038
Abbotsford, BC V2T 3T8
604-850-6639

Burnaby Family Life Institute
32-250 Willingdon Avenue
Burnaby, BC V5C 5E9
604-659-2200

Burnaby Multicultural Society
6255 Nelson Avenue
Burnaby, BC V5H 4T5
604-431-4131

**Campbell River and Area Multicultural
and Immigrant Services Association**
43-1480 Dogwood Street

Campbell River, BC V9W 3A6
250-830-0171

Chilliwack Community Services
45938 Wellington Avenue
Chilliwack, BC V2P 2C7
604-792-4267

Comox Valley Family Service Association
1415 Cliffe Avenue
Courtenay, BC V9N 2K6
250-338-7575

Cowichan Valley Intercultural and Immigrant Aid Society
3-83 Trunk Road
Duncan, BC V9L 2N7
250-748-3112

Kamloops Cariboo Regional Immigrant Services Society
110-206 Seymour Street
Kamloops, BC V2C 2E5
250-372-0855

Multicultural Society of Kelowna
100-1875 Spall Road
Kelowna, BC V1Y 4R2
250-762-2155

Langley Family Services Association
5339-207th Street
Langley, BC V3A 2E6
604-534-7921

Central Vancouver Island Multicultural Society
114-285 Prideaux Street
Nanaimo, BC V9R 2N2
250-753-6911

**Lower Mainland Purpose Society
for Youth and Families**
40 Begbie Street
New Westminster, BC V3M 3L9
604-526-2522

North Shore Multicultural Society
102-123 East 15th Street
North Vancouver, BC V7L 2P7
604-988-2931

Penticton and District Multicultural Society
508 Main Street
Penticton, BC V2A 5C7
250-492-6299

Immigrant and Multicultural Services Society of Prince George
1633 Victoria Street
Prince George, BC V2L 2L4
250-562-2900

Richmond Multicultural Concerns Society
210-7000 Minorou Boulevard
Richmond, BC V6Y 3Z5
604-279-7160

Family Services of Greater Vancouver
250-7000 Minorou Boulevard
Richmond, BC V6Y 3Z5
604-279-7100

Richmond Connections
190-7000 Minorou Boulevard
Richmond, BC V6Y 3Z5
604-279-7020

Surrey Delta Immigrant Services Society
1107-7330 137th Street
Surrey, BC V3W 1A3
604-597-0205

Options: Services to Community
100-6846 King George Highway
Surrey, BC V3W 4Z9
604-596-4321

Progressive Intercultural Community Services Society
109-12414-82nd Street
Surrey, BC V3W 3E9
604-596-7722

Family Services of the North Shore
101-255 West 1st Street
Vancouver, BC V7M 3G8
604-988-5281

Immigrant Services Society
530 Drake Street
Vancouver, BC V6B 2H3
604-684-7498

Collingwood Neighbourhood House
5288 Joyce Street
Vancouver, BC V5R 6C9
604-435-0323

Jewish Family Service Agency
300-950 West 41st Avenue
Vancouver BC V5Z 2N7
604-257-5151

Kiwassa Neighbourhood House
2425 Oxford Street
Vancouver, BC V5K 1M7
604-254-5401

Little Mountain Neighbourhood House
3981 Main Street
Vancouver, BC V5V 3P3
604-879-7104

MOSAIC
1522 Commercial Drive, 2nd Floor
Vancouver, BC V5L 3Y2
604-254-9626

The People's Law School
150-900 Howe Street
Vancouver, BC V6Z 2M4
604-688-2565

Ray-Cam Cooperative Centre
920 East Hastings Street
Vancouver, BC V6A 3T1
604-257-6949

Riley Park Community Association
50 East 30th Avenue
Vancouver, BC V5V 2T9
604-257-8641

South Vancouver Neighbourhood House
6470 Victoria Drive
Vancouver, BC V5P 3X7
604-324-6212

SUCCESS
28 West Pender Street
Vancouver, BC V6B 1R6
604-684-1628

Frog Hollow Neighbourhood House
2131 Renfrew Street
Vancouver, BC V5M 4M5
604-251-1225

Hispanic Community Centre
Society of BC
4824 Commercial Street
Vancouver, BC V5N 4I1
604-872-4431

Pacific Immigrant Resources Society
385 South Boundary Road
Vancouver, BC V5K 4S1
604-298-4560

Vancouver Association for the Survivors of Torture (VAST)
3-3664 East Hastings Street
Vancouver, BC V5K 2A9
Tel: 604-299-3539

West End Community Centre Association
870 Denman Street
Vancouver, B.C. V6G 2L8
604-257-8333

Vernon and District Immigrant Services
100-3003 30th Street
Vernon, BC V1T 9J5
250-542-4177

Victoria Immigrant and Refugee Centre
305-535 Yates Street
Victoria, BC V8W 2Z6
250-361-9433

Intercultural Association of Victoria
930 Balmoral Road
Victoria, BC V8T 1A8
250-388-4728

CHAPTER - III

STRATEGIZING FOR EMPLOYMENT IN THE CANADIAN WORKPLACE

"A Journey of a 1000 Miles Begins with a Single Step" Lao Tzu

Bio – IRENA VALENTA

As a career development practitioner, Ms. Valenta maintains 6 years of professional practice in the areas of adult vocational assessment, career management, job placement, work search, labour market research and workforce development. Ms. Valenta's background includes 12 years experience in counseling with children and families.

Ms. Valenta's professional development includes:

- Current Certification and Membership as a Life Skills Coach - Association of Life Skills Coaches, Ontario
- Current membership with the Ontario Association of Career Development Practitioners, Ontario
- Adult Training and Development program - OISE, University of Toronto, Toronto, Ontario
- Diploma in Career and Work Counseling - George Brown College, Toronto, Ontario
- Masters Degree in Social Work - McGill University, Montreal, Quebec

Currently, Ms. Valenta is working as manager/facilitator of a Job Finding Club program funded by Human Resources Development Canada and operated by The Career Foundation (www.careerfoundation.org).

Ms. Valenta's focus and goal is to incorporate labour market research as an integral and creative skill in career management.

Toronto, Ontario, Canada

WHY STRATEGIZE?

The Canadian Workplace Reality

Job search in Canada is no longer a matter of completing an application form and hoping for a job offer. Canadian businesses involved in technological innovation, corporate restructuring and unpredictable fluctuations in the recent global economy can no longer guarantee a job for life for you.

How people work is changing and so are occupational titles. Individuals are encouraged to look for work that matches their personal values and talents. The term "job" has transformed into "meaningful work" which is planned and has personal value in addition to the monetary compensation.

The onus is on the job seeker to research, to track and to secure employment options. These job opportunities may materialize as contract jobs, part-time jobs, "work-from-home" jobs, job sharing arrangements, casual assignments and long term arrangements –or any combination thereof. To ensure your financial security, you need to constantly market your expertise to potential consumers of service.

Many internationally educated professionals in Canada have described barriers to enter their career after their arrival in Canada. The acculturation process may create such scenarios as:

- You may not necessarily achieve your career goals immediately
- You may have to take the time to gain Canadian accreditation for your professional credentials
- You may have to settle for alternative employment in the short-term to accommodate your life style and to upgrade your English language skills
- You may have to upgrade your technical skills on your own time to become employable in your field of interest.

Personal career management has become the responsibility of the individual worker who is expected to continuously create employment opportunities in keeping with a focused and planned career path.

Become a Career Strategist

In order to successfully manage your career and financial security, it is not enough to be a "job seeker" who depends on advertised vacancies as was done in traditional job search. The career strategist knows him/herself, knows the world of work, is a lifelong learner and creates his/her own work opportunities on an ongoing basis. Career planning has evolved into work/life planning –an entrepreneurial process which involves more creative thinking and risk-taking on the part of the individual.

To gain personal control and confidence in an unpredictable workplace, the following concepts are important to keep in mind:

Essential Concepts to Remember in Work Search*

- Employment opportunities depend on the current supply of work and demand for workers in the Canadian labour market
- There is an abundance of information on the changing Canadian labour market to chart your work search campaign
- Technology impacts all occupations most of which require skilled workers
- Ongoing research of labour market information is a vital skill to be learned for career planning and employment search

---

Due to the necessity of constant change and the demands of the Canadian economy, many new work opportunities are being created.

Be prepared to work differently: to contribute your ideas, to take initiative

The key tasks to become a career strategist may include:

1. Identify and diversify your career vision to give you purpose and direction in securing employment

2. Consistently re-assess and upgrade your technical and employability skills to help you to remain employable in the short-term and the long range

3. Networking and researching labour market information to keep you updated on trends in Canadian industries and occupations so that you can align your opportunities to the requirements of the job market.

4. Conduct a personal job search campaign by developing strategic job search documents and self-marketing techniques

5. Access Canadian on-line career resources and free community-based employment services to benefit from free information and support in your search for employment

6. Adopt a customer service philosophy in order to present your skills as a solution to current business demands.

---

*O'Reilly, Elaine. *Making Career Sense of Labour Market Information*. Canadian Career Development Foundation. HRDC British Columbia Ministry of Advanced Education. 2001. www.workinfornet.bc.ca

THE STRATEGY to discover work opportunities......

As a career strategist, you first need to answer the following questions:

- What skills do I have to offer the Canadian labour market?
- Where will the jobs be?
- What competencies do Canadian employers look for in a worker?
- How do I market myself effectively to potential employers?
- Which free employment services may assist me in the community?

The next steps will be to formulate and maintain a **Plan of Action**:

- people to contact
- places to go to
- things to do
- questions to ask regarding your work search in Canada.

Your success in the workplace will be determined by the initiative, time and effort you invest in your professional and personal vision.

SOME WEBSITES to strategize your research.....

The following websites have been organized and categorized in order to present options for you in your work research and career strategizing efforts.

1. Assess what skills and strengths YOU as a unique individual have to offer to the Canadian labour market?

> ### *Know your Skills, Values, Interests and Personality Preferences*
>
> *http://www.cdm.uwaterloo.ca* Career Development eManual, University of Waterloo, Ontario
>
> *http://www.jobhuntersbible.com* Online supplement to Richard Bolles "What Color is Your Parachute?" → Tests & Advice

2. Discover the current Canadian Labour Market Trends

Which industries are growing? Where are the jobs?

www.labourmarketinformation.ca Government of Canada

http://www24.hrdc-drhc.gc.ca HRDC Sector Studies & Partnerships → Canadian Industry profiles

www.jobsetc.ca Government of Canada → Jobs, Workers, Training & Careers

http://www.canadaprospects.com Canadian Career Consortium, Career awareness, career planning and work search programs

http://www.strategis.gc.ca Industry Canada, Canada's business & consumer site

http://www.canadainternational.gc.ca Government of Canada, services for non-Canadians

www.councils.org The Alliance of Sectoral Councils → Directory of products & services related to growth industries in Canada. Funded by Human Resources Development Canada.

www.skillscanada.com Resources for careers in the skilled trades in Canada

www.statcan.ca Statistics Canada → The Daily, Labour Force Survey

www.tradesway.com HRDC & Centre for Education and Training→Search Newcomers

---

3. Find out about Canadian COMPANIES

Service/Product, corporate culture, networking contacts, job postings & career resources.

www.sedar.com Canadian public company profiles

www.ctidirectory.com Canadian Trade Index, Canadian Manufacturers & Exporters

www.cdnbusinessdirectory.com Canada Business Directory
www.cbr.ca Canadian Business Resource, Database of Canadian corporate profiles

www.newswire.ca Canadian database of news releases

www.yellowpages.ca National & local business directory

http://vts.ic.gc.ca Industry Canada, Virtual Trade Show on Information & Communication technologies and company profiles

www.corporateinformation.com International corporate profiles

www.infomart.ca Canadian news & business information on-line, Industry Profiles & Corporate Data

4. Learn more about Canadian OCCUPATIONS

> ### *Job requirements & descriptions, projected growth & related occupations*
>
> http://www23.hrdc-drhc.gc.ca/2001/e/generic/welcome.shtml
> HRDC, National Occupational Classification
>
> http://jobfutures.ca Human Resources Development Canada,
> Job Futures 2002 → Occupations and Want to Immigrate?
>
> http://www.careerccc.org/careerdirections/eng/e_ho_set.htm
> Canada Career Consortium, Canadian occupations not
> requiring university education
>
> www.cicic.ca Canadian Information Centre for International
> Credentials →Information on Specific Occupations and Trades
>
> http://www.equalopportunity.on.ca/eng_g/apt/index.asp
> Government of Ontario, Gateway to Diversity, Internationally
> Trained Workers, Access to Professions & Trades
>
> www.madewiththetrades.com Careers in the construction
> industry
>
> http://www.red-seal.ca HRDC, Interprovincial Standards Red
> Seal Program for trades, apprenticeships and skilled workers

5. Know the SKILLS, WHICH may make you more employable

What are the interpersonal skills that Canadian employers are expecting from all job seekers in addition to technical skills?

http://www.careerccc.org/destination2020 Canada Career Consortium, Build your Work Skills

http://www.conferenceboard.ca/education/learning-tools/esp20 The Conference Board of Canada, Employability Skills 2000+

http://www15.hrdc-drhc.gc.ca HRDC, Essential Skills for Life Learning and Work

http://www.psc-cfp.gc.ca/research/personnel/ei_e.htm Emotional Intelligence in the Workplace, Human Resource Management Trends & Issues, Public Service Commission of Canada

http://www.canadaone.com/magazine/eq080498.html Emotional Intelligence and the New Workplace, CanadaOne Magazine, free on-line magazine for small business in Canada

6. Prepare to MARKET YOUR SKILLS to Canadian employers

Effective job search documents & self-marketing techniques

http://www.workinfonet.ca – Jobs, work & recruiting. Canada WorkInfonet Partnership.

http://www.worksearch.gc.ca Human Resources Development Canada, work search strategies

www.monster.ca Canada's career management portal

www.rileyguide.com Online resource for employment & career information

www.quintcareers.com Career & job portal

7. Identify which Free Community Services are available to assist you to live and work in the Canadian workplace?

Employment & settlement services

http://www.hrdc-drhc.gc.ca/dept/guide/jwtc.shtml Human Resources Development Canada Offices – Jobs, Workers, Training & Careers

www.SEECanada.Org Gateway to Settlement, Employment & Education for skills professionals & Tradespersons planning to immigrate to Canada

www.poss.ca Human Resources Development Canada, Toronto's Virtual Employment Resource Centre

www.settlement.org Information & resources for immigrants to Ontario. Citizenship & Immigration Canada Employment

---

8. Prepare for PROFESSIONAL DEVELOPMENT

Standards of Practice, networking & career resources

www.careerkey.com Career networking resource on-line – Links – Associations

www.cicic.ca/profess-enphp Canadian Information Centre for International Credentials – national professional organizations

http://www.charityvillage.com/charityvillage/profas.asp Professional associations in the non-profit sector

http://circ.micromedia.on.ca/hotlinks/associations/main.htm Associations Canada

http://info.asaenet.org/gateway/OnlineassocSlist.html American Society of Association Executives, directory of associations

---

9. If you need SOME ADDITIONAL INFORMATION, try 0consulting with an on-line career resource person :

Free on-line career consultation & information

www.workopolis.com – Career Resources – Immigrate to Canada – New Canadian Advisor

www.CanadaInfoNet.org Canadian mentors for professionals, business & skilled trades people considering immigrating to Canada

---

TOP 40 INTERVIEW QUESTIONS

1.   Tell me about yourself?
2.   Tell me about any of your weakness?
3.   What are some of your strengths?
4.   Where do you see yourself in 5 years?
5.   What work experience have you had that prepares you for this position?
6.   Why should we hire you?
7.   Do you consider yourself a creative problem solver? Give me an example.
8.   Why did you leave your last position?
       Why did you leave your last position?
9.   Your resume shows you have moved around a lot. How can I be sure you will stay at this company?
10.   What did you think of your last supervisor/manager?
11.   Describe your ideal position.
12.   What did you like about your last job?
13.   What did you dislike about your last job?
14.   Describe how you work under pressure.
15.   Describe your ideal boss.
16.   What do you have to offer this company that others may not?
17.   What kind of salary are you looking for?
18.   What was your annual salary at your last position?
19.   What have you gained from working at your last job?
20.   What were your responsibilities and duties?
21.   What motivates you?
22.   Do you consider yourself successful?
23.   What traits or qualities do you most admire in someone?
24.   What are your hobbies?
25.   Are you willing to relocate?
26.   Tell me about your proudest accomplishment?
27.   What has been your most meaningful educational experience?

28. Can you tell me something about our company.

29. Describe how you perform in a high stress position?

30. How do you feel about routine work?

31. What steps are you taking to improve yourself?

32. Do you have a personal goal that you still want to achieve?

33. Tell me about what you would do to get organized for a project.

34. Have you ever been responsible for financial management?

35. There is a period of time on your resume when you were not employed. Can you tell me what you did in that time period?

36. Would it be appropriate to contact your most recent employer?

37. What do you think will be the most difficult aspect of this job?

38. What are your expectations from our organization

39. What special skills / talents do you have?

40. Do you have any questions for me? (usually at the end of interview)

Note: When you will visit your nearest Human Resource Centre In Canada you will find many books on interview questions with their answers and some even with specific professions. You will also find many books on resume writing.

INTERVIEW PRACTICE - AN EXAMPLE

Practicing for the interview means practicing several behaviours – not just answering questions. You must dress well, watch your body language and posture, practice your manners and eye contact, as well as practice answering questions correctly, smoothly and with confidence.

The practice questions below, in one form or another, account for a large percentage of interview questions. With each question, you are given a series of choices as to how you might answer the question. When you select an answer, you will learn to whether your answer is correct or not - and why. Answering these questions will help you polish your interviewing techniques. The questions and answers in this exercise are generic and in many cases, must be tailored to your individual situation. Still, the logic behind the answer remains essentially the same.

1. Why are you the best person for the job?

(a) "I've held a lot of positions like this one and that experience will help me here."

(b) "Because I am good at what I do."

(c) "Our discussion here leads me to believe this is a good place to work."

(d) "You need someone who can produce results and my background and experience are proof of my ability. For example…"

2. If asked a point blank question such as: Are you creative? Are you analytical? Can you work under pressure? Etc. what is the best way to answer?

(a) Answer yes or no.

(b) Answer yes and give a specific example.

(c) Answer yes and give an explanation.

3. Describe yourself.

(a) Outline personal data, hobbies and interests.

(b) Give an overview of your personality and work habits.

(c) Give three specific examples of your personality traits and accomplishments.

4. Why are you in the job market?

(a) "I have invested a great deal of time with my company and become disenchanted with the ways things are done".

(b) "I have a solid plan for my career. Within that plan I am looking for additional responsibility and more room for growth."

(c) "I have been passed over for promotions when I know I am capable of doing more. I want to move on to a company that will not stunt my growth."

5. What are you looking for in a position?

(a) "I'm looking for an opportunity to apply my skills and contribute to the growth of the company while helping create some advancement opportunities for myself ".

(b) "I'm looking for an organization that will appreciate my contributions and reward my efforts."

(c) "I'm looking for a position that will allow me to make enough money to support my lifestyle. I am a hard worker and will give a concerted effort to earn the money I need."

6. What do you know about our organization?

(a) "I've done a little homework and here is what I know about your organization... (cite examples)."

(b) "Everything I've seen and heard makes me want to be a part of this organization. I understand your industry is _____ and your primary customer is _____. A particularly exciting part of your business appears to be_____

(c)   "I know enough to know this is an exciting place to work. It appears to be fit for my career goals."

7.   What are your strengths?

(a)   "I am good at giving constructive criticism to my co-workers. This honesty is something I'm very proud of and have found essential to having open working relationships."

(b)   "I consider myself to be very consistent. I have proven myself to be someone who can be counted upon to do what is expected."

(c)   "I would have to choose between two skills. I am very proud of my determination and ability to get things done. At the same time I am very proud of my analytical abilities and problem solving skills These skills combine to give me a unique ability to solve problems and then implement the solutions."

8.   Why haven't you taken a job yet?

(a)   "I've talked to a number of people, but it is very difficult to find an organization that is the right fit."

(b)   "I've come across a few attractive opportunities but, so far. I haven't found a position that pays what I feel I am worth."

(c)   "I have done some careful planning because this decision is very important to me. I have been offered positions but, to date, I have not been able to find a position that meets my criteria and this is important because the match must be good for me as well as the company. The position we are discussing today appears to be a good fit."

9.   Where do you see yourself in five years?

(a)   "In five years, I will have either been promoted to your job or have started my own business."

(b)   "This is a very volatile market. I find it difficult to project out five years."

(c)   "That really depends on the firm I join. I would like to take a position with some responsibility and room for growth. The key is with the right challenge, I intend to continually contribute and grow with the firm."

10.   Before we go any further, what kind of money do you need to make?

(a)   "I was making 50K at my last job and I feel I am worth at least 10 % more."

(b)   "The current job market shows a salary range of $____ to $____ for this type of position. However, my salary requirements are negotiable. Your firm has a reputation of compensating employees fairly and I trust you would do the same in my case. I am very interested in finding the right opportunity and will be open to any fair offer when I do so."

(c)   "Money is not very important to me. I need to be able to pay the bills, but the work environment is far more important to me."

CONCLUSION

The purpose of this article is to provide some focus and some preliminary on-line career resources to research for internationally trained workers who are considering employment in Canada. Being prepared with career-specific information and an action plan for work search in Canada will, hopefully reduce the potential barriers often faced by newcomers.

I also hope that this career strategy will contribute to a less stressful and more successful journey in work and life in Canada.

To read this article in your language, you may wish to access the following free web-based translation services:

♦ www.freetranslation.com

♦ http://world.altavista.com

♦ http://www.google.com/language_tools?hl=en

Note: Every effort has been made to ensure that the resources listed in this article were correct at the time of printing. Any errors or omissions in the data are due to an oversight on my part and are not intended to mislead or misinform professionally or legally.
(Irena Valenta - Toronto, Ontario, Canada)

SOME USEFUL ADDRESSES

Medical Council of Canada (MCC)
P.O. Box 8234, Station T
Ottawa, Ontario K1G 3H7
Canada

Tel.: (613) 521-6012
Fax: (613) 521-9417
http://www.mcc.ca/
Rev. Date: 3/14/2002 6:31:56 PM

Canadian Council of Technicians and Technologists (CCTT)
285 McLeod Street
Ottawa, Ontario K2P 1A1
Canada

Tel.: (613) 238-8123
Fax: (613) 238-8822
Email: ctabadm@magma.ca
http://www.cctt.ca/
Rev. Date: 5/29/2002 10:33:47 AM

Canadian Institute of Chartered Accountants (CICA)
227 Wellington Street West
Toronto, Ontario M5V 3H2
Canada

Tel.: (416) 977-3222
Fax: (416) 977-8585
Email: qualification.reform@cica.ca
http://www.cica.ca/
Rev. Date: 3/22/2002 4:59:27 PM

Certified General Accountants Association of Canada (CGA-Canada)

1188 West Georgia Street, Suite 700
Vancouver, British Columbia V6E 4A2
Canada

Tel.: (604) 669-3555 or 1-800-663-1529
Fax: (604) 689-5845
Email: public@cga-canada.org
http://www.cga-canada.org/
Rev. Date: 2/13/2002 10:05:56 AM

Society of Management Accountants of Canada (CMA-Canada)
One Robert Speck Parkway,
Suite 1400 P.O. Box 176
Mississauga, Ontario L4Z 3M3
Canada

Tel.: (905) 949-4200 or 1-800-263-7622
Fax: (905) 949-0038
Email: info@cma-canada.org
http://www.cma-canada.org/
Rev. Date: 1/31/2002 11:43:51 AM

List of Associations Of Professional Engineers

Alberta

Association of Professional Engineers, Geologists and
Geophysicists of Alberta (APEGGA)
10060 Jasper Avenue 1500 Scotia One
Edmonton, AB T5J 4A2
Canada

Tel.: (780) 426-3990 or 1-800-661-7020
Fax: (780) 425-1722
http://www.apegga.org/

British Columbia

Association of Professional Engineers and Geoscientists of
British Columbia (APEGBC)
200-4010 Regent Street

Burnaby, BC V5C 6N2
Canada

Tel.: (604) 430-8035 or 1-888-430-8035
Fax: (604) 430-8085
http://www.apeg.bc.ca/

Manitoba

Association of Professional Engineers and Geoscientists of
Manitoba (APEGM)
850A Pembina Highway
Winnipeg, MB R3M 2M7
Canada

Tel.: (204) 474-2736
Fax: (204) 474-5960
http://www.apegm.mb.ca/

New Brunswick

Association of Professional Engineers and Geoscientists of New
Brunswick (APEGNB)
535 Beaverbrook Court, Suite 105
Fredericton, NB E3B 1X6
Canada

Tel.: (506) 458-8083
Fax: (506) 451-9629
http://ctca.unb.ca/apenb/

Newfoundland and Labrador

Association of Professional Engineers and Geoscientists of
Newfoundland (APEGN)
10 Fort William Place,
Suite 203, P.O. Box 21207
St. John's, NF A1A 5B2
Canada

Tel.: (709) 753-7714
Fax: (709) 753-6131
http://www.apegn.nf.ca/

Northwest Territories

Association of Professional Engineers, Geologists and Geophysicists of the Northwest Territories (NAPEGG)
201, 4817-49th Street
Yellowknife, NT X1A 3S7, Canada

Tel.: (867) 920-4055
Fax: (867) 873-4058
http://www.napegg.nt.ca/

Nova Scotia

Association of Professional Engineers of Nova Scotia (APENS)
1355 Barrington Street, P.O. Box 129
Halifax, NS B3J 2M4
Canada
Tel.: (902) 429-2250 or 1-888-802-7367
Fax: (902) 423-9769
http://www.apens.ns.ca/

Ontario

Professional Engineers of Ontario (PEO)
25 Sheppard Avenue West, Suite 1000
Toronto, ON M2N 6S9
Canada
Tel.: (416) 224-1100 or 1-800-339-3716
Fax: (416) 224-8168 or 1-800-268-0496
http://www.peo.on.ca/

Prince Edward Island

Association of Professional Engineers of Prince Edward Island (APEPEI)
549 North River Road

Charlottetown, PE C1E 1J6
Canada

Tel.: (902) 566-1268
Fax: (902) 566-5551
http://www.apepei.com/

Québec

Ordre des ingénieurs du Québec (OIQ)
2020, rue University, 18e étage
Montréal, QC H3A 2A5
Canada

Tel.: (514) 845-6141 or 1-800-461-6141
Fax: (514) 845-1833
http://www.oiq.qc.ca/

Saskatchewan

Association of Professional Engineers and Geoscientists of Saskatchewan (APEGS)
2255-13th Avenue, Suite 104
Regina, SK S4P 0V6
Canada

Tel.: (306) 525-9547 or 1-800-500-9547
Fax: (306) 525-0851
http://www.apegs.sk.ca/

Yukon

Association of Professional Engineers of Yukon (APEY)
3106 Third Avenue, Suite 404, P.O. Box 4125
Whitehorse, YT Y1A 5G1
Canada

Tel.: (867) 667-6727
Fax: (867) 668-2142
http://www.apey.yk.ca/

Canadian Council of Professional Engineers (CCPE)
180 Elgin Street, Suite 1100
Ottawa, On K2P 2K3
Canada

Tel.: (613) 232-2474
Fax: (613) 236-5759
Email: ia@ccpe.ca
http://www.ccpe.ca/
Rev. Date: 2/19/2002 11:52:27 AM

Ordre des ingénieurs du Québec (OIQ)
2020, rue University, 18e étage
Montréal, PQ H3A 2A5
Canada

Tel.: (514) 845-6141 or 1-800-461-6141
Fax: (514) 845-1833
Email: admission@oiq.qc.ca
http://www.oiq.qc.ca/
Rev. Date: 2/19/2002 12:12:39 PM

Provincially-mandated Evaluation Services

Alberta

International Qualifications Assessment Service
Alberta Learning
4th Floor, Sterling Place
9940 - 106 Street
Edmonton, Alberta   T5K 2V1   Canada

Tel: (780) 427-2655; Fax: (780) 422-9734
E-mail: iqas@gov.ab.ca
http://www.learning.gov.ab.ca/iqas/iqas.asp

British Columbia

International Credential Evaluation Service
4355 Mathissi Place
Burnaby, BC V5G 4S8
Canada

Tel: (604) 431-3402
Fax: (604) 431-3382
E-mail: ICES@ola.bc.ca
http://www.ola.bc.ca/ices/

Manitoba

Academic Credentials Assessment Service - Manitoba (ACAS)
Manitoba Labour and Immigration
Settlement & Labour Market Services Branch
5th Floor, 213 Notre Dame Avenue
Winnipeg, Manitoba, R3B 1N3
Canada

Tel: (204) 945 - 6300 or (204) 945 - 5432
Fax: (204) 948 - 2148
E-mail: glloyd@gov.mb.ca
http://www.immigratemanitoba.com

Ontario

World Education Services-Canada
45 Charles Street East, Suite 700
Toronto, Ontario M4Y 1S2
Canada

Tel.: (416) 972-0070
Fax: (416) 972-9004
Toll-free: (866) 343-0070 (from outside the 416 area code)
Email: ontario@wes.org
http://www.wes.org/ca/

Quebec

Service des équivalences (SDE)
Ministère des Relations avec les citoyens et de l'Immigration
800, boulevard de Maisonneuve Est, 2e étage
Montréal (Québec) H2L 4L8
Canada.

Tél: (514) 864-9191 ou (877) 264-6164;
Fax: (514) 873-8701
Email:equivalences@mrci.gouv.qc.ca
http://www.immq.gouv.qc.ca/equivalences

Other Evaluation Services

Academic Credentials Evaluation Service
Office of Admissions, Room 150, Atkinson College
York University
4700 Keele Street
Toronto, Ontario M3J 1P3
Canada

Tel.: (416) 736-5787;
Fax: (416) 736-5536
E-mail: dstadnic@yorku.ca
http://www.yorku.ca/admissio/aces.asp

Comparative Education Service
University of Toronto
315 Bloor Street West,
Toronto, Ontario M5S 1A3
Canada

Tel: (416) 978-2185; Fax: (416) 978-7022
http://www.adm.utoronto.ca/ces/

International Credential Assessment Service of Canada
147 Wyndham Street North, Suite 409
Guelph, ON N1H 4E9
Canada

Tel: (519) 763-7282
Toll-free: (800) 321-6021
Fax : (519) 763-6964
Email: icas@sympatico.ca
http://www.icascanada.ca/

Note: Evaluation services have an appeal process in place for individuals who wish to challenge the assessment of their credential.

Labour Market Information
by Province and Territory

Canada is a large and diverse country. Job opportunities and labour market conditions are different in each region. It is important to obtain labour market information about the area where you want to live. Most provinces and territories provide information on their labour markets.

Alberta

Alberta Learning
7th Floor, Commerce Place
10155 102 Street
Edmonton, Alberta T5J 4L5 Canada

Telephone: 780-427-7219
Toll-free access, first dial 310-0000.
Fax: 780-422-1263
E-mail: comm.contact@learning.gov.ab.ca
URL: www.learning.gov.ab.ca/welcome/English/pdf/Employment.pdf

British Columbia

Aboriginal, Multiculturalism and Immigration Programs
PO Box 9214
Stn Prov Gov't
Victoria, British Columbia V8W 9J1 Canada

Telephone: 250 952-6434
Fax: 250 356-5316
URL: www.gov.bc.ca/mi/popt/movingtobc.htm

Manitoba

Immigration and Multiculturalism Division
5th floor - 213 Notre Dame Avenue
Winnipeg, Manitoba R3B 1N3, Canada

Telephone: (204) 945-3162
Facsimile: (204) 948-2256
Email: immigratemanitoba@gov.mb.ca
URL: www.gov.mb.ca/labour/immigrate/newcomerservices/8.html

New Brunswick

Investment and Immigration,
Department of Business New Brunswick
P O Box 6000
Fredericton, New Brunswick E3B 5H1, Canada

Telephone: (506) 444-4640
Facsimile: (506) 444-4277
E-mail: immigration@gnb.ca
URL: www.gnb.ca/immigration/english/work/work.htm

Ontario

Access to Professions and Trades Unit
Ministry of Training, Colleges and Universities
12th Floor, 900 Bay Street, Mowat Block
Toronto, Ontario M7A 1L2, Canada

Telephone: (416) 326-9714
Facsimile: (416) 326-6265
E-mail: aptinfo@edu.gov.on.ca
URL: www.equalopportunity.on.ca/eng_g/apt/index.asp

Prince Edward Island

Immigration and Investment,
Development and Technology
94 Euston Street 2nd Floor
Charlottetown, PEI C1A 1W4 Canada

Telephone: (902) 894-0351
Facsimile: (902) 368-5886
URL: www.gov.pe.ca/infopei/Employment/index.php3

Quebec

**Ministère des Relations avec les citoyens
et de l'Immigration (MRCI)**

How to reach us:
www.immigration-quebec.gouv.qc.ca/anglais/reach.html
Email: Renseignements.DRM@mrci.gouv.qc.ca
URL: www.immigration-quebec.gouv.qc.ca/anglais
/services/insertion_en.html

Saskatchewan

Saskatchewan Government Relations and Aboriginal Affairs
8th Floor, 1919 Saskatchewan Drive
Regina, Saskatchewan S4P 3V7 Canada

Email: immigration@iaa.gov.sk.ca
URL: www.iaa.gov.sk.ca/iga/immigration/Immigration.htm
(Accreditation and Services sites under development)

Yukon

Labour Market Program and Services -
Department of Education
Advanced Education Branch
Box 2703 Whitehorse, Yukon Y1A 2C6 Canada

Telephone: (867) 667-5141 or
Toll Free: 1-800-661-0408
Facsimile: (867) 667-8555

Ontario Association of Certified Engineering Technicians and Technologists (OACETT)
10 Four Seasons Place
Suite 404
Etobicoke M9B 6H7 Ontario
Canada

Tel: (416) 621-9621
Fax: (416) 621-8694
E-Mail: info@oacett.org

Other Technical Associations

The Association of Engineering Technicians and Technologists of Newfoundland Inc. (AETTN)
P.O. Box 790
22 Sagona Ave, Unit # 1, Donovan's Industrial Park
Mount Pearl, Newfoundland, A1N 2Y2,
Canada

Tel: 709-747-2868
Fax: 709-747-2869
E-Mail: Registrar@aettn.com

Association of Certified Engineering Technicians and Technologist of Prince Edward Island (ACETTPEI)
c/o PEISCET
P.O. Box 1436
Charlottetown, PE C1A 7N1
Canada

Tel: (902) 892-TECH (8324)
Fax: (902) 566-9394
E-mail: info@peiscet.pe.ca

Society of Certified Engineering Technicians and Technologist of Nova Scotia (SCETTNS)
Belmont House
33 Alderney Drive, Suite 425
Dartmouth, NS B2Y 4P5
Canada

Tel: (902) 463-3236
Toll Free: 1- 866 - SCETTNS (723-8867)
E-Mail: scettns@ns.sympatico.ca

New Brunswick Society of Certified Engineering Technicians and Technologists (NBSCETT)
115 - 535 Beaverbrook Court
Fredericton, New Brunswick
E3B 1X6
Canada

Tel: (506) 454-6124
Toll Free: 1-800-665- TECH
Fax: (506) 452-7076
E-mail: nbscett@nbscett.nb.ca

L'Ordre des technologues professionnels du Québec
1265, rue Berri, bur.720
Montréal (Québec) H2L 4X4
Canada

Tél. (514) 845-3247 ou 1-800 561-3459
Fax (514) 845-3643
E-Mail: admission@otpq.qc.ca

Certified Technicians and Technologists Association of Manitoba (CTTAM)
602 - 1661 Portage Avenue
Winnipeg, Manitoba, R3J 3T7
Canada

Phone: (204) 784-1088
Fax: (204)784-1084
E-mail: admin@cttam.com

Saskatchewan Applied Science Technologists & Technicians (SASTT)
363 Park Street, Regina,
SK. S4N 5B2
Canada

Tel: (306) 721-6633
Fax: (306) 721-0112
E-mail: sastt@sk.sympatico.ca

Alberta Society of Engineering Technologists (ASET)
2100 - 10104 103 Ave NW (Bell Tower),
Edmonton, Alberta T5J 0H8
Canada

Tel: 780-425-0626 or toll free within Alberta 1-800-272-5619
Fax: 780-424-5053
E-mail: asetadmin@aset.ab.ca

Applied Science Technologist and Technicians of British Columbia (ASTT)
10767 - 48th St
Surrey, BC V3R 0S4
Canada

Tel: (604) 585-2788
Fax: (604) 585-2790
E-Mail: techinfo@asttbc.org

Consulting Engineers of Ontario
405 - 10 Four Seasons Place
Toronto, ON M9B 6H7
Canada
Tel: 416-620-1400
Fax: 416-620-5803
E-mail: staff@ceo.on.ca

Ontario Good Roads Association
530 Otto Road, Unit 2
Mississauga, ON L5T 2L5
Canada
Tel: 905-795-2555
Fax: 905-795-2660

Ontario Association of Home Inspectors (OAHI)
Box 38108 Castlewood R.P.O.
Toronto Ontario M5N 3A8
Canada
Tel: 416-256-0960
Toll Free: 888-744-6244 / E-Mail: oahi@oahi.com

LIST OF SUGGESTED JOB SEARCH WEB SITES

Canada Job search	www.canadajobsearch.com
Canada Wide	www.canada.com
Canada Work Info Net (B)	http://workinfonet.ca
Canada Work Infonet	www.workinfonet.com
Canadian Career Page	www.canadiancareers.com
Career Bookmarks	www.careerbookmarks.tpl.toronto.on.ca
Career Exchange	www.creerexchange.com
Career Mosaic	www.careermosaic.com
Career Networking	www.careerkey.com
Contractors Network Corporation	www.cnc.ca
Culture Net Announcement Board	www.culturenet.ca
Electronic Labour Exchange	www.ele-spe.org
E-Span	www.espan.com
Head Hunter	www.HeadHunter.net
HEART/Career Connections	www.career.com
Hot Jobs	www.hotjobs.com
HRDC Canada(B)	www.hrdc-drhc.gc.ca
Job Bus Canada	www.jobbus.com
Job Find	www.jobfind2000.com
Job Hunters Bible	www.jobhuntersbible.com
Job Search Canada	www.jobsearchcanada.about.com
Job Search Engine	www.job-search-engine.com
Job Shark	www.jobshark.com
Monster Board	www.monster.ca
Net Jobs	www.netjobs.com
Ontario Government (B)	www.gojobs.gov.on.ca
Public Service Commission of Canada(B)	http://jobs.gc.ca
Toronto HRDC Jobs and Links	www.toronto-hrdc.sto.org
University of Toronto Job Board	www.utoronto.ca/jobopps
Work Search (B)	www.worksearch.gc.ca
Workink(B)	www.workink.com
Work Insight	www.workinsight.com
Workopolis	www.workopolis.com

HI TECH

Hi Tech Career Exchanges	www.hitechcareer.com
IT Career Solutions	www.vectortech.com
Position Watch	www.positionwatch.com
Ward Associates	www.ward-associates.com

ENGINEERING

Canadian Society for Mechanical Engineers	www.csme.ca
Engineering Institute of Canada	www.eic.ici.ca

NON PROFIT ORGANIZATION

Canadian International Development Agency	www.acdi-cida.gc.ca
Charity Village	www.charityvillage.com
Human Rights-Job Bank	www.Hri.ca/jobboard/joblinks.shtml
Law Now's Resource for Charity/Non Profit	www.extension.ualberta.ca/lawnow/nfp
Online Resource for Non Profit	www.onestep.on.ca

HEALTH

Canadian Medical Placement Service	www.cmps.ca
Hospital News	www.hospitalnews.com
Med Hunters	www.medhunters.com

EDUCATION

Jobs in the Educational Field	www.oise.utoronto.ca/~mpress/jobs.html

WOMEN

Wired Woman	www.wiredwoman.com

MULTI MEDIA

MultiMediator	www.multimediator.com

TOURISM AND HOSPITALITY

Cool Jobs Canada	www.cooljobscanada.com
Hospitality Careers	www.hcareers.com

AGRICULTURE

Caffeine	www.caffeine.ca
The Farm Directory	www.farmdirectory.com/employment.asp

ARTS AND ENTERTAINMENT

Acting	www.madscreenwriter.com
ACTRA (film)	www.actra.com
Canadian Actor Online	www.canadianactor.com
Canadian Actors Equity Association	www.caea.com
Canadian film @ TV Production Association	www.cftpa.ca
Canadian Film Centre	www.cdnfilmcentre.com
Mandy	www.mandy.com
National Film Board	www.nfb.ca
Ontario Theatre	www.theatreontario.org
Playback Magazine	www.playbackmag.com

SPECIALIZED

Canadian Federation of Chefs & Cooks	www.cfcc.ca
Canadian Human Resource Counsellors	www.chrp.ca
Contact Point – Counsellors	www.contactpoint.ca
Oil and Gas Industry	www.pcf.ab.ca
Social Workers of Toronto	www.swatjobs.com

PEOPLE WITH DISABILITIES

Canadian Council for Rehabilitation & Work	www.ccrw.org
Canadian Hearing Society	www.chs.ca
Canadian Mental health Association	www.cmha.ca
Canadian Paraplegic Association	www.canparaplegic.org
Job Accommodation Network	http://janweb.icdi.wvu.edu
TCG for People with Disabilities	www.tcg.on.ca
U of T Adaptive Tech ERC	www.utoronto.ca/atrc

WEB SITES FOR YOUTH AND RECENT GRADUATES

Bridges	www.bridges.com
Canadian Youth Business Foundation	www.cybf.ca

Canadian Youth Business Foundation (B)	www.cybf.ca
Career Owl	www.careerowl.ca
Career Planning	www.alis.gov.ab.ca
Cdn.International Development Agency (B)	www.acdi-cida.gc.ca
Federal Student Work Experience Program (B)	www.jobs.gc.ca
MazeMaster	www.mazemaster.on.ca
National Graduate Register	http://ngr.schoolnet.ca
Strategies Business Info – By Sector (B)	Strategis.ic.gc.ca/sc_indps/engdoc/homepage.html
Summer Jobs	www.summerjobs.com
Work Web (B)	www.cacee.com
Youth Canada (B)	www.youth.gc.ca
Youth Info-Job (B)	www.infojob.net
Youth Opportunities Ontario (B)	Youthjobs.gov.on.ca
Youth Opportunities Ontario (B)	www.edu.gov.on.ca

NEW COMERS

Citizenship and Immigration Canada	www.cic.gc.ca
Settlement.org	www.sttlement.org
Skills for change	www.skillsforchange.org
World Educational Services/Foreign Credentials Assessment	www.wes.org/ca

CAREER PLANNING AND JOB SEARCH STRATEGIES

Bridges	www.cxbridges.com
Career Cruising	www.careercruising.com
Counselor Resource Centre (B)	http://crccanada.org
Essential Skills	www.essestialskills.gc.ca
Job Futures	http://jobfutures.ca
National Occupational Classification (NOC)(B)	www.hrdc.gc.ca/noc
Toronto Public Library	http://careerbookmarks.tpl.vrl.toronto.on.ca
What Colour is your parachute:	www.jobhuntersbible.com

LABOUR MARKET / INDUSTRY INFORMATION

Canada News Wire	www.newswire.ca
Canada Work InfoNet (B)	www.workinfonet.ca
HRDC Metro Toronto(B)	www.toronto-hrdc.sto.org
HRDC Sector Studies (B)	www.on.hrdc-drhc.gc.ca/english/lmi
Industry Canada	http://strategis.ic.gc.ca
Labour Market Information: Salary Ranges	www.Canadavisa.com/documents/salary.htm
Ontario Wage Information	www.on.hrdc-drhc.gc.ca

NEWSPAPERS/MAGAZINE

Eye Magazine	www.eye.net/classifieds.
Globe and Mail	www.theglobeandmail.com
National Post	www.careerclick.com
Newswire	www.neweswire.ca
Toronto Star	www.thestar.com
Toronto Star / Globe and Mail	www.workpolis.com
Toronto Sun	www.canoe.ca

SMALL BUSINESS INFORMATION

Business Development Bank of Canada (B)	www.bdc.ca
Canada Business Service Centres (B)	www.cbsc.org
Canadian Company Capabilities (B)	Strategis.ic.gc.ca/engdoc/main.html
Canadian Women's business Network	www.cdnbizwomen.com
Educated Entrepreneur	www.educatedentrepreneur.com
Enterprise Toronto	www.enterprisetronto.com
Self Employment Assistance	http://www.sedi.org/html/prog/fs1_prog.html
Toronto Business	www.city.toronto.on.ca/business/index.htm

WEB SITES WHERE YOU CAN POST YOUR RESUME

Electronic Labour Exchange	www.ele-spc.org
Job Canada	www.jobcanada.org
Job Shark (B)	www.jobshark.com
Monster Board (B)	www.monster.ca
National Graduate Register (B)	www.campusworklink.com
NetJobs	www.netjobs.com
Worklink	www.workink.com
Workopolls	www.workopolis.ca

TRAINING

Can Learn	www.canlearn.ca
Ellis Chart/Apprentice Training Programs	www.hrdc.gc.ca/hrib/hrpprh/redseal/ndex.shtml
Interactive Training Inventory (B)	www.trainingiti.com
Ministry of Education & Training	www.edu.gov.on.ca/eng/welcome.html
Onestep	www.onestep.on.ca
Ontario Universities' Application Centre	www.ouac.on.ca
Scholarships and Exchanges (B)	www.homer.aucc.ca
School finder(B)	www.schoolfinder.com

TUTORIAL SITES

Internet Stuff	www.webteacher.com
Learn the Net	www.learnthenet.com
Microsoft Office: word, excel, powerpoint	www.utexax.edu/cc/training/handouts
Mouse Tutorial	www.albright.org/Albright/computer-Lab/tutorials/mouse/

RELEVANT INFORMATION

City of Toronto	www.city.toronto.on.ca
Employment Resource Centres	www.tcet.com/ercs
Possibilities Project	www.possibilitiesproject.com

VOLUNTEER SITES

Charity Village	www.charityvillage.com
Rehabilitation	www.voc-reb.org
Volunteers	www.volunteer.ca

FREE EMAILS SITES

Excite	www.excite.com
Hotmail	www.hotmail.com

Mail City	www.mailcity.com
Yahoo	www.yahoo.com

SINGLE SEARCH ENGINES

www.google.com	www.altavista.com
www.excite.com	www.go.com
www.hotbot.com	www.yahoo.ca

META SEARCH ENGINES

www.search.com	www.profusion.com
www.megaweb.com	www.metacrawler.com
www.dogpile.com	

Please Note

This publication contains information that was current at the time of publication. It features information from many sources, and should not be confused with official statements of policy or programming. The Government of Canada is not responsible for information that changes between printings.

About the Author

The Author is a Mechanical Engineer and Cisco Certified Network and Design professional (CCNP, CCDP, A+) with more then 14 years of experience in his field of expertise with multi-national companies especially in Middle East. He arrived in Canada as an immigrant and faced numerous surprises and challenges as well as suffering a number of losses.

The Author has a flare to help and teach, he wishes to save new immigrants from potential losses and miseries by sharing the wealth of information that he has gathered while immigrating and settling in Canada. After interviewing hundreds of new immigrants from various countries, the author has come to the conclusion that the root cause of all the problems and loss of hard earned money is the lack of information before arriving in Canada.

So by compiling this publication he is giving everything to new or potential immigrants to access their eligibility under every immigration class and submit their immigration application by themselves in a professional manner. Also start working towards their eligibility for employment in Canada and explore or secure a job offer or small business while their cases are in process.

The Author can be reached at *tariq_nadeem@sympatico.ca* for advise or feedback upon his publication.

He has compiled this publication with the approval of Citizenship and Immigration Canada (CIC) and with the authorization of Communication Canada, Ottawa, Ontario K1A 1M4

Lightning Source UK Ltd.
Milton Keynes UK
10 March 2010

151220UK00002B/78/A